Managing Your Classroom

with Heart

A Guide for Nurturing Adolescent Learners

Katy Ridnouer

ASCD

Association for Supervision and Curriculum Development
Alexandria, Virginia USA

Association for Supervision and Curriculum Development
1703 N. Beauregard St. • Alexandria, VA 22311 1714 USA
Phone: 800-933-2723 or 703-578-9600 • Fax: 703-575-5400
Web site: www.ascd.org • E-mail: member@ascd.org
Author guidelines: www.ascd.org/write

Gene R. Carter, Executive Director; Nancy Modrak, Director of Publishing; Julie
Houtz, Director of Book Editing & Production; Katie Martin, Project Manager;
Catherine Guyer, Senior Graphic Designer; Circle Graphics, Typesetter; Vivian Coss,
Production Specialist

ASCD Member Book, No. FY07-3 (December 2006, P). ASCD Member Books mail to
Premium (P), Comprehensive (C), and Regular (R) members on this schedule: Jan.,
PC; Feb., P; Apr., PCR; May, P; July, PC; Aug., P; Sept., PCR; Nov., PC; Dec., P.

PAPERBACK ISBN-13: 978-1-4166-0462-4   ASCD product #107013
PAPERBACK ISBN-10: 1-4166-0462-6
Also available as an e-book through ebrary, netLibrary, and many online booksell-
ers (see Books in Print for the ISBNs).

Quantity discounts for the paperback edition only: 10–49 copies, 10%; 50+ copies,
15%; for 1,000 or more copies, call 800-933-2723, ext. 5634, or 703-575-5634. For desk
copies: member@ascd.org.

Library of Congress Cataloging-in-Publication Data

Ridnouer, Katy.
    Managing your classroom with heart : a guide for nurturing adolescent
learners / Katy Ridnouer.
        p. cm.
    ISBN-13: 978-1-4166-0462-4 (pbk. : alk. paper)
    ISBN-10: 1-4166-0462-6 (pbk. : alk. paper)
    1. Classroom management. 2. Teenagers–Education. 3. Teacher-student
relationships. I. Title.

    LB3013.R526 2006
    371.102'4—dc22
                                                                        2006025718

17 16 15 14 13 12 11 10 09 08 07 06   1 2 3 4 5 6 7 8 9 10 11 12

*For Terry McCaffery, my omnipresent
source of encouragement and care;
Mike and Marilyn Ridnouer, my everyday
inspirations; and Sean, James, and
Will McCaffery, my daily teachers of
innumerable lessons.*

Managing Your Classroom with Heart

A Guide for Nurturing Adolescent Learners

Introduction

Although the United States trains more than enough teachers to meet its needs, the attrition rate for educators is higher than that of any other professional occupation. According to a report from the National Commission for Teaching and America's Future, up to one-third of new U.S. teachers leave the profession within the first few years.* I was one of them.

In my second year, I taught 8th grade language arts in a school full of challenges. I felt isolated, unsafe, and incapable, but I trudged on. I met with parents, I brainstormed with colleagues, and I discussed issues with members of the administration. Nothing changed. At the end of the year, I decided to leave teaching for the quiet solitude of the bookseller's life.

For six months or so, I convinced myself that I had made a good choice. Then the dreams about my classroom started. I was in front of my 8th graders, leading a grammar lesson. I saw their willing faces. I saw *them*. I then realized that I had expected everyone else to change while I remained the same. I expected the surly child to be pleasant, but I did nothing to encourage this behavior. I expected the underachieving child to work to his potential, but I did nothing

---

*Fulton, K., Yoon, I., & Lee, C. (2005, August). *Induction into learning communities*. Washington, DC: National Commission for Teaching and America's Future. Available: 2100 M Street, NW, Washington, DC 20037. http://www.nctaf.org.

to bring this about. I even expected the motivated child to stay motivated but did nothing to contribute to that end. My eyes opened, I returned to teaching and I have never looked back.

I identify as a teacher. It's what I am meant to do, and it is as rewarding to me as art is to the artist, a great play is to the athlete, and the correct diagnosis is to the doctor. When I see students grapple with a concept and come away with new understanding of the material and a new respect for themselves, the long hours I invest hardly matter.

Although I found my way back to the classroom, many others do not. And when nearly half of all new teachers leave the classroom by the end of their fifth year, it creates a cumulative loss of experience for our schools and our communities. We lose the practical skills a teacher can acquire only by working with students; we lose the insights gained by connecting with students from varied backgrounds; and we lose the passion of someone who set out to change children's lives.

What can be done to decrease the attrition rate? What can be done to encourage teachers to stay? What can be done to make teaching as rewarding and fulfilling as we hoped it would be when we first decided to walk this path? This book is my response to these questions, based on my own experience. I have worked with many professionals who love to teach but are so frustrated that they have left the profession for some peace of mind. I know how frustrating it can be to attempt a task to which you're absolutely committed and yet still meet with failure day after day.

The kids whose stories I tell in this book attended an urban high school where minority students receiving free or reduced lunch comprised 40 percent of the student body. On the other end of the spectrum, 15 percent of the students were white and from affluent families. This disparity contributed to a tense environment that only furthered my determination to change the way I approached teaching.

Today, my guiding maxim as a teacher is to create a learning community within the four walls of the classroom. I define a learning community as a group of people who come together with a willing spirit to learn and support one another despite racial, economic, religious, and achievement differences. Learning communities promote curiosity, higher-level thinking, enhanced interpersonal skills, and confidence in both students and teachers. I have found that the key to creating a learning community is to *manage your classroom with heart*—and by that, I mean permeate the classroom atmosphere with caring concern. This involves care in interactions with students, lesson planning, seating chart decisions, discipline concerns, grading, and more. Putting your care for your students first creates a learning community that inspires them to be their best selves, both in school and out in the world.

When I went back to the classroom, I changed the way I perceived my job. Instead of trying to be a commander, I became a facilitator. A commander issues orders that have been handed down from the higher-ups and does so without much thought to the students involved; a facilitator creates guidelines that help her understand her students so she can find a way to help them meet curricular goals—a way that takes account of their background, of who they are, and of what else is going on in their lives. To become a facilitator, I had to change the way I responded to student behaviors that bothered me. I had to accept that my students would have worldviews different from mine, and I had to accept that the difference was a good thing.

Most significantly, I had to care about my students, which was something I hadn't really allowed myself to do before. Sure, I was friendly to them and I wanted them to succeed, but I can't say I was a caring teacher. Frankly, I saw caring as a risky venture. I worried that my feelings might be hurt if my students mocked my concern for them or if they didn't reciprocate it. I worried that I might get caught up in my students' personal concerns and neglect their academic achievement. I worried that the administration would think I had "gone soft." But on my second go-round, I decided to take the risk: to allow myself to care about my students—to nurture them and their learning. I am a happier teacher, a better teacher, and a richer human being because of it. My great hope is that by welcoming my students into my heart, I have enriched their lives. My hope for you, reading this book, is that you and your students will be enriched through your own caring concern.

Students know who they can and can't learn from. My first year back, I began asking my students to fill out an anonymous survey at the end of the year as a way to help me gauge the type of teacher-student interaction that is the most beneficial. The survey went on to become an annual ritual, and I've reproduced a copy of it in Figure 1.

The first question the survey asks students is whether they can learn from a teacher they dislike. Every year, the students over-whelmingly reply no. The next question on the survey asks them to describe how a teacher they disliked made them feel about themselves. Here's a sample of the kind of responses I get:

- "Like no matter how much I tried, I would still fail his class."
- "Slow, dumb, and like a troublemaker."
- "A little helpless, because I did not know how to do the work."
- "She didn't make me feel anything. I have no interest in the subject and I don't really care about the teacher."
- "He made me feel as if his class was too hard for me."
- "I used to feel bad, but through different situations and maturity, I saw I am me and whatever I want to be I can be, regardless."
- "He makes me feel like I am not even there, and that he doesn't have time to answer a silly question I might have."
- "This teacher makes me feel like chopped liver. I don't think I can remember a time where I've been so embarrassed to go into a class. I feel like I do not even matter."

As you see, these responses are full of hostility, lowered self-worth, anxiety, shame, and anger. The only positive one involves a student who was able to think highly of herself *in spite of* the teacher.

The next question asks the students to describe the teacher they dislike. Here are some typical responses:

- "She gives no help, cannot control the class, and is quick to kick people out."

Figure 1
Survey

1. Can you learn from a teacher you dislike? Why or why not?

2. How did a teacher you dislike make you feel about yourself?

3. Describe a teacher you dislike (no names, please!).

4. Can you learn from a teacher you care about? Why or why not?

5. How did a teacher you care about make you feel about yourself?

6. Describe a teacher you care about.

- "He acts like he doesn't have time for extra help when you don't understand."
- "She's all in your face, like you're doing well, socializing with you, but you're not doing well."
- "I don't think that he likes black students."
- "Crabby, cranky, always gives busy work, whiny, mean, only here for job, doesn't care about *us,* our feelings, our future."
- "She notices that you are struggling, but doesn't try to help."
- "Insults you or makes you feel lower than them. Will not let you voice your opinion in a calm way. Piles you down with work and then doesn't grade it."

These teachers chose to show negative sides of their personalities. At least, it's the negative side that lingers in the memories of these students, who saw them 48 minutes a day, 5 times a week, and 180 days a year—plenty of time to collect and store an opinion of these professionals assigned to guide their learning lives. Some of these students resolved that they just had to "get over not liking the teacher." Instead of focusing on learning the subject matter, which any professional teacher would agree should be all students' top priority, these kids were preoccupied with learning how to get along with the teacher. I do not believe these teachers would like to be seen in this fashion, especially given the possibility that students were not learning precisely because of their negative perceptions of these teachers.

Then the survey asks students to describe a teacher they care about. Again, their responses do not vary much:

- "She really shows that she cares about her work and her students."
- "She stays on my back and makes me want to learn."
- "She is calm, nice, and loves astronomy."
- "She shares her intelligence with me."
- "She takes me step by step and makes it fun."
- "She gives me confidence that she knows I can do or achieve something. She tells me I'm doing a good job and that she knows I'm going to make it in the future."

- "She's nice and wants you to learn and earn good grades. All jokes aside until the time is right."
- "She makes you enjoy her class."
- "The teachers that I love most are funny and they feel comfortable in a student atmosphere. Yet work is being accomplished at the same time."

Yes, the overall quality that these students are responding to is *care*. They love the teachers who care about them; that feeling overflows into their attitude toward themselves as learners and, ultimately, into their attitude toward the subject matter.

Next, the survey asks students to describe how the teacher they care about makes or made them feel about themselves. Here's a look at how they respond:

- "Like I was smart and bright."
- "Like if I listen, pay attention, and put some effort into it, I can do the work."
- "Like I was somebody."
- "Glad that I signed up for the course."
- "Like I could learn anything."
- "Confident."
- "She makes me feel good about myself because she told me it was OK to make mistakes as long as you learn from them."

The feeling of self-worth these students' comments express is a bridge to any kind of success. When these students believed in themselves, they found that each of their subjects was easier.

Years of student responses to this survey have convinced me that it is essential to accept students as they are and to make sure they know that we care about them enough to provide the structure and support that will help them grow. If we nurture all students as individuals, they become more confident and gain a better sense of who they are and what they want out of life. The budding scientists, dancers, journalists, business owners, musicians, and CEOs need to communicate their dream for their future with someone who cares about them and will help them achieve that dream. Even a math teacher with a student who is an artist in the making can recognize her gifts, call her "the future artist," and inform her of upcoming art shows. By caring for and about every student, we increase the odds of our students' personal and professional success tremendously.

I have seen myself how caring for students helps a teacher meet curricular goals; tapping into the excitement of reaching a child emotionally provides energy to reach that child academically. Try out the many approaches that I illustrate throughout this book, and you will find yourself concentrating less on "dealing with" your students and more on inspiring them. It is my hope that as you put my guidelines into practice, you will begin to develop your own classroom management style—one that's a perfect fit for both your personality and your school. This book is intended as a starting point. Your final destination is entirely up to you.

1

Choosing to Care

> *There are only two ways to live your life. One is as though nothing is a miracle. The other is as though everything is a miracle.*
>
> —Albert Einstein

Teaching adolescents is a tough job. Those of us who enter the profession with glorious visions of intellectual conversations and quiet, industrious classrooms soon realize that these come only through lots of hard work, convincing, and cheerleading.

We also find that being a teacher involves much more than teaching a subject. Our job is to educate the population we have been given to teach: to teach these particular students to learn and to learn about themselves. Before we begin to think about curriculum, we must make a connection with our students and establish a classroom environment in which they feel safe, physically and intellectually. We must convince them that we will protect them in this way, and we must help them be physically comfortable enough to access their intellect.

There are many obstacles that can stand in the way of this connection, including age difference, economic difference, values difference, and attitude difference. As professionals, we have to make it our job to recognize these obstacles, plan for them, and deal with them. When we bridge the gaps and connect with our students—when we manage our classrooms with heart—we move closer to the vision of the teacher we want to be and the classroom we want to have. Once students know that we care about them, that we are on their team, they will learn any grammar rule and read any book.

A Look into an Uncaring Classroom

Trust in yourself. Your perceptions are often far more accurate than you are willing to believe.

—Claudia Black

Every day at lunch, Ms. Hall mutters, "I can't stand them. They think they're cute, but they're not. Not in the least."

She never expected to dread her fourth period sophomore English class this way. She readily admits that one of her students, James, controls the classroom. James has ADHD and comes from a troubled home. He is also really smart. Ms. Hall complains that nothing works to "shut James up." When the rest of the class is discussing the previous day's reading, he regularly interrupts with stories from his own life.

Today is no different.

"Yesterday we continued our reading of *The Pearl*," says Ms. Hall, beginning the day's lesson. "What seemed to be something that could bring great joy, now seems to be wreaking havoc on the family. As we—"

"Ms. Hall, I was thinking that this novel is a lot like my own life," James interrupts.

"Well, that's no surprise, James," Ms. Hall replies, "but we do not have the time to talk about that right now."

"Oh, it'll just take a minute," James promises.

Ms. Hall relents, and James begins.

"Well, you know how in the story Kino beats his wife? Well, my mom is telling her lawyer that my dad beats her and *that's* why she wants a divorce. She also figures it will help her alimony case. Well, I told my dad what my mom was planning. Now he's even madder at her, and he says she will only get *half* of everything now, just like the law says. And now my mom is pissed at me because she overheard me on the phone with my dad talking about where I'd like to live. I made a joke about how he might hit me if I didn't live with him. Well, my dad thought it was funny, but my mom sure didn't. Now I'm staying with my dad until my mom cools off. Weird, huh?"

"Yeah, weird," agrees Ms. Hall. She is careful to keep her voice even and hide her growing impatience. "But, James? I do not see how that relates to *The Pearl*. Let's get back to the lesson now, OK?"

Cynthia raises her hand.

"Yes, Cynthia. You have something to contribute?"

"Ms. Hall, what happened to James has happened to me too."

"No, Cynthia, we really don't—"

"It'll only take a minute!" Cynthia insists, and then continues with her story.

Some of the students are pleased that they have gotten off task, but others can see Ms. Hall's anger mounting. By the time Cynthia is finished, Ms. Hall cannot contain it any longer. "Cynthia, did you just waste five minutes of class time to tell us about your grandmother's lungs? Why does this matter to us? How does it relate to *The Pearl*? I'll know better than to call on you next time."

"Ms. Hall, my story is certainly more interesting than this crap by Steinbeck," Cynthia retorts.

"You know you cannot talk to me like that," Ms. Hall points out.

"I just did," Cynthia says.

"I would never in my life have spoken to a teacher in the way you have just spoken to me!"

"You were disrespectful to me, so I'm disrespectful to you."

Ms. Hall sighs deeply. She rubs her eyes and runs her fingers through her hair, the same hair the kids love to ask her questions about. ("How long does it take to dry?" "Why don't you ever wear it down?" "Is that your natural color?") She remembers this and thinks, *annoying, annoying, annoying.* Then she says, "You know, this is supposed to be an advanced class."

She now has almost everyone's attention. But not James's. "Can I go to the bathroom?" he interrupts.

"*May I,* you mean, and yes, you may," Ms. Hall answers wearily. "Get the pass off my desk."

James jumps up, taps a girl on the head, grabs the pass, and twirls out of the class. The students are in hysterics. Ms. Hall is furious.

"OK, is that what you want? You want to watch a foolish child leap around because he can't hold it for another 25 minutes until class is over? You guys are on your own. Silently—that means no noise—*silently,* I want you to read to page 95 and then tell me how the pearl is affecting the decisions that the family has to make. I want three paragraphs, in ink, turned in at the end of the period. This is for an essay grade."

"Ms. Hall, you want us to read 15 pages *and* write an essay in 25 minutes? You're nuts!" Tommy calls out. His classmates murmur their agreement. For Ms. Hall, this is the last straw.

"That's it! Tommy, go to lockout. I'm sick of you kids being so disrespectful. What can I do to teach you not to be so disrespectful? Never mind. You're in the 10th grade; you should know how to behave."

Tommy has not moved.

"Tommy, go!" Ms. Hall commands.

"Why should I? I just said what everyone is thinking," Tommy responds.

"Oh, you know best," she says, rolling her eyes. "Just stay seated and do your work."

"I need a book," Lynda says.

"Me too," says Mary.

"Oh, yeah, my mom left mine on the kitchen counter," says Ronnie.

"You guys know I don't have extras. How can we do silent reading if you can't bring your books?" Exasperated, Ms. Hall pairs the students up, ignoring the whispers and the note writing. The class settles into a low hum. Just three students are actually working on the assignment.

Ms. Hall goes to her desk in the back of the room. Just as she sits down, James walks in, saying, "You wouldn't believe what someone—"

Ms. Hall interrupts James with a loud "Shhh! Sit down and do the assignment."

"What's the assignment?" James asks. "Oh, and does anybody else need the pass?"

"James, *I* tell people if they can use the pass or not, not you," Ms. Hall says.

"I need it, Ms. Hall. I have to call home. It's an emergency," Tonda says, unconvincingly.

Ms. Hall hands Tonda the pass and then tells James, "Read to page 95 and then write a three-paragraph essay about how the pearl is affecting the decisions that the family is making."

"We're not going to read out loud? Come on. Who wants to read out loud?" James asks, looking around for votes.

"Yeah, Ms. Hall. We'll never be able to read this on our own," Latisha chimes in.

"You guys are pitiful," Ms. Hall says, but she relents. "OK. Out loud. James, you start on page 80."

"But I'm already on page 85. That's not fair," says Stephen, who has been working conscientiously.

"You will just have to start over with us or continue reading on your own," Ms. Hall replies.

Stephen scowls and pulls out his math book to start his home-work for that class.

The rest of the students lean over their books and pretend to be following along with James. Ms. Hall makes no attempt to define the words that she suspects are unfamiliar, and she does not stop to ask questions to gauge how well the students are understanding the novel. She keeps her eyes on her book. James reads on.

Finally, the bell rings. "Do the essay for homework!" Ms. Hall yells over the ringing.

Caring as an Avenue to Teaching

It is not because things are difficult that we do not dare; it is because we do not dare that they are difficult.

—Seneca

Ms. Hall acknowledges that these students are, in fact, "advanced" students, yet when they try to create a connection from their lives to the story, she becomes frustrated. She doesn't recognize the value of their sharing their personal lives. A caring teacher realizes that behavior that is a distraction often provides insight into the students' needs and personal situations. In this case, Ms. Hall could have used the information her students had volunteered to enrich the lesson plan and strengthen classroom relationships. James was the first student to cause a disruption. Ms. Hall knows that James has a lot going on in his life. Although she hears the story that James tells about his home situation, she does not pick up on the desire to feel understood that lies beneath it. By listening attentively to his story, she is telling him that his use of class time is valid; and yet, she does nothing to try to connect his story with the lesson.

Ms. Hall could meet James's needs by actually listening to his words and picking up on the energy he uses to tell the story. If she had taken the time to do that, the situation might have gone like this:

Ms. Hall: James, it sounds to me like you feel torn choosing between your mother's side and your father's side.

James: Yeah. It's hard, you know? I'm an only child. I don't have a brother or a sister to talk to.

Ms. Hall: So it's easy to see your home situation in every part of your life. So much so that when you read that Kino beat his wife, you thought of your mom. . . .

James: Yeah. I do that a lot when I read. I see stuff that goes on in my life in the story that I'm reading. Is that weird?

Ms. Hall: Class, what do you think? Is it weird to connect your own life with what you read?

In this scenario, Ms. Hall connects with James and reframes his behavior as a connection to a curriculum-related topic. "How life and literature mix" can be a difficult concept for students to grasp, but James's concrete example is a great illustration. Ms. Hall's sympathetic response to James makes it more likely that other students in the class will be willing to contribute honestly to a discussion of this topic.

This same sort of approach could be used with Cynthia, who sees a similarity between her grandmother's life and the life of the novel's main character but cannot quite verbalize it. Does Ms. Hall see Cynthia's story as a potential bridge to the novel's content? Does Ms. Hall help Cynthia step up to make that connection? No. Ms. Hall gets angry because Cynthia did not make her story relevant to the lesson. Here's another, much more positive way Ms. Hall could have responded:

Ms. Hall: I understand that your grandmother is a really strong person who didn't give in when she was a child. But I'm having a hard time seeing how Kino is like your grandma.

Cynthia: My grandma had such a hard life for such a long time, and she made it even worse by smoking.

Ms. Hall: By smoking?

Cynthia: Yeah! She can't go anywhere without an oxygen tank, and nobody will hire her with that thing. She's been on welfare for 20 years.

Ms. Hall: And how is her life like Kino's?

Cynthia: Well, Kino's life was never great, just like my grandma's wasn't ever great, but she used to able to *breathe* at least. Kino loved his wife. He didn't beat her, I mean. That is, until the pearl came along and ruined everything.

Ms. Hall: In your grandma's life, what do you see as similar to the pearl?

Cynthia: The cigarettes. The cigarettes ruined her life, like the pearl ruined Kino's. She thought smoking would make her look glamorous and attract wealthy men. She spent her time try-ing to look good instead of educating herself. The knight in shining armor never came, but the lung cancer sure did.

Ms. Hall: Now I see your connection with the book. Kino allowed the pearl to dictate his actions, like your grandmother allowed the cigarettes to dictate hers. So, what are some things in our own lives that are like the pearl? This question is open to the class. . . .

In this alternative scenario, Cynthia is validated both emotionally and intellectually. And again, the rest of the class also benefits because this real-life example of a situation similar to that in the novel gives them another way to relate personally to the story.

A second problem in this classroom is that it's not the teacher but the *students* who are in charge. Students today have mastered the art of manipulating the direction of a lesson by acting out or changing the subject; they knock the teacher off track, and the teacher has a difficult time getting back to the point. Ms. Hall has fallen into this trap. More than likely, James doesn't really need to go to the bathroom. He's on autopilot; when the classroom gets dull, he finds a way to get out. Ms. Hall is left seething, but she is too angry to recall what she was saying prior to his interruption.

When students do this, we have to recognize it for what it is: an attempt at control. Students want to feel that they are in a controlled environment. I do not mean a dictatorship type of control, but a *managed* control, where reasonable, logical thinking reigns. If the teacher is not controlling the class, the class will control itself. Ms. Hall needs to recognize this. She needs to stop and assess the situation: *This is James. He always asks to use the restroom, but I need to finish what I'm saying.* She might then just look at James and raise her index finger to indicate "just a minute please," telling James that she has heard him but that he will have to wait until she has a spare moment. Doing this also sends the rest of the class the message that interruptions are not acceptable and that the teacher is in control. This helps Ms. Hall maintain a calm classroom where the students feel they can let down their guard and listen to what she is saying. When Ms. Hall does return to James and allows him to go to the restroom, he will have had time to calm down too. Perhaps he won't act out on his way out the door. If he does,

Ms. Hall might inform him that she needs to speak with him privately in the hall when he returns. This tells James that his *behavior* is unacceptable but that he himself is worthy of respectful treatment. It also tells the class that their teacher does not tolerate this unacceptable behavior.

With a little more effort, Ms. Hall could eliminate the other students' off-task behavior through closer monitoring. After giving the reading assignment, she might give students a minute or two to get out their books and become settled, but then she should insist on quiet because that is what is needed for this activity. As students work, Ms. Hall might walk around the classroom looking for off-task behavior, including students writing personal notes, talking with seatmates, or working on homework from another class. She might give students who are off task a squeeze on the shoulder or a steady look in the eyes—providing correction but not embarrassment. The students are likely to show their appreciation by cooperating. Ms. Hall might also read along silently with the students or make herself available by being in their direct line of vision. This monitoring also sends a message that she is serious about the assignment. And if James makes a noisy re-entrance, Ms. Hall could simply direct him to go back outside and accompany him for a little chat, keeping the door cracked so that she can peek in to check on the class but still ensure privacy in her dealings with James.

James needs to know how his behavior makes his teacher feel. Often, students are unaware that they are irritating someone else. The dialogue might proceed like this:

Ms. Hall: James, the way you interact in my class tells me that I've given you the wrong idea about how I want you to behave.

James: What do you mean?

Ms. Hall: I mean, I've told you not to interrupt me or anyone else, but I haven't always ignored your interruptions the way I should have. If I had done a better job of that, you'd know that you were interrupting. Maybe you would learn to think before you speak and perhaps raise your hand when you have something to add.

James: I never thought about it like that.

Ms. Hall: I also must be too tolerant of your goofy behavior because otherwise you wouldn't make such a scene entering and exiting the class.

James: Oh, that's just me. I always do that.

Ms. Hall: It frustrates me when you do it because instead of the students working on English, they are laughing at you.

James: True. I don't mean to make you frustrated. I'm just in it for the laugh, you know?

Ms. Hall: I know, and that's normal. Still, could you try to be calm and quiet when I do allow you to leave the classroom? I would appreciate it.

James: I'll try, but I might need a reminder.

Ms. Hall: No problem. OK, let's go back into the room.

In this conversation, James is validated that he is a normal person, but he just needs to tone down his behavior. He has also had the opportunity to see Ms. Hall as a person—not as a ranting teacher who is annoyed that he is controlling the class yet again. The other students see James walking in quietly and a calm look on Ms. Hall's face. The show is over and everything's OK. They have nothing left to do but get back to work.

Questions for Reflection

1. What can you do to show that you care for your students?
2. What student behaviors get under your skin?
3. What are your negative emotional reactions to these behaviors?
4. How might you reframe these behaviors to change your negative emotional reactions to positive reactions?
5. How might this reframing enhance your students' understanding of the lesson?

2

Interacting with Students

The greatest thing a human being ever does in this world is to see something. To see clearly is poetry, prophecy, and religion; all in one.

—John Ruskin

Many of us believe that if we were "good" teachers, we would never be emotional in the classroom, would never allow our personal lives to spill over into our professional lives, and would never be caught in situations where we are unsure or do not know the answer. These "nevers" not only are unrealistic but also rob us of our humanness. Signing a 10-month teaching contract and filling out a grade book does not negate the fact that we are fallible. We need to clear out the "nevers" so that we can interact with our students in ways that are honest and real.

Being "real" with students pays off in both curricular and interpersonal ways. When I share my frustrations and my joys in the classroom, my students connect with me because they see that I am human too. Because they know I am not perfect and will not chastise them for their own imperfections, they are more willing to take risks: to offer their interpretations of a piece of literature or chance misreading a line of Shakespeare.

Sharing ourselves occasionally with the students we teach also offers them a chance to show their own emotional and intellectual maturity. Once, following a negative experience with an administrator, I told my students that I especially appreciated their "good mornings" because I was having a frustrating day. They also picked up that my fuse was a little shorter than usual and showed me that they understood this. Another time, when I was reading three different pieces of literature with my three different levels of classes and could not recall a minute detail about one of the novels, I didn't try to hide this from my students. Instead, I told them what I was doing in my other classes and admitted that perhaps I had bitten off more than I could chew. Not only did they understand, but a few even volunteered to be the class experts on the novel—the ones we could all look to when we needed to find a certain part of the reading.

I am certainly not saying that teachers should talk about their emotional states, their outside business, and their occasional gaps in knowledge all the time. Remember, though, that students are perceptive, especially teenage ones. When you are feeling strain, they know it, and they're usually ready with biting comments: "Hey, what's up with you?" "You need to calm down." "Ms. Ridnouer, *you* don't know the answer? Then how do you expect me to?"

There are several ways a teacher might respond:

- "Nothing is up with me. And if there was, it wouldn't be any of your business."
- "I need to calm down? *I* don't need to do anything. *You* need to shut your mouth."
- "Since when is it OK to be so disrespectful to a teacher?"

These are all honest, human reactions. But the challenge we face is to step outside the situation and see these moments of conflict for what they are: *a chance to connect.* This requires a level of maturity and self-awareness that many adults have yet to achieve. It's a level not guaranteed by the award of a teaching certificate. We, as professionals responsible for shaping the minds of later generations, need to be honest with ourselves and work toward this maturity and self-awareness for our students' sake.

A classroom is like a ship. Someone does have to be in command, but a captain who verbally whips and publicly abuses his crew will soon be watching his back whenever he nears the plank. I don't want to have to watch my back in my own classroom. I like that the vast majority of my students seem to respect me. I like that I can trust them to do what I ask them to do and that I can trust nine-tenths of them to do what a *substitute* asks them to do when I'm not around. This kind of respect and trust is not automatic and can't be assumed from day one. It's not a function of me being the adult or of me being the teacher, who "knows best" and "deserves" respect. It is something that must be developed over time: constructed, tested, and reconstructed.

Four Guidelines for Interacting with Students

> *What a gift of grace to be able to take the chaos from within and from it create some semblance of order.*
> —Katherine Paterson

How do you build a caring classroom—one that allows you to teach the lesson and model positive behavior? Here are four guidelines that are the backbone of my interactions with students. They provide a way to manage a classroom in a manner that is mature and professional and yet makes connection and care possible.

Guideline #1: Don't let students fast-talk you

You know fast-talk when you hear it. It's the avalanche of reasons a student presents to explain why he or she has not done the homework, is tardy, needs an extension, and so on. Teachers who let themselves be "fast-talked" are those who allow themselves to be worn down or swayed by these excuses. To stop this student from talking, or to express relief that the student has finally *stopped* talking, they let the student slide with a warning for "next time." Having met with the success, the student repeats the same process the next time an opportunity presents. Then other students, who have witnessed this winning ploy, begin to try it themselves. The teachers are left wondering why there is chaos in their classrooms.

Here is the approach I recommend when a student is trying to use fast-talk to slide through a rule. Let the student speak, and when she stops, look her square in the face and hold her gaze with your eyes. If the fast-talk starts up again, keep holding her gaze and raise your hand in a "stop" position. Then repeat the rule, and end with, "If you need to discuss this further, come see me after class." Repetition is key, as is stating your rules as a matter of fact: "Late homework is marked down 10 percent." "If you don't have a pass when you are late, you are marked." "The due date is set." "Late work is marked down one letter grade."

Guideline #2: Stay focused on the problem

It is very easy to get upset when a student talks back, speaks disrespectfully, or disrupts the class. Often, instead of addressing the actual problem, we address our emotional response to the problem. This can turn into a rant that actually prolongs the class disruption. Another unintended consequence is that the student who started the problem is never disciplined according to class rules.

Acknowledge the student's complaint by repeating what he has said, if that is appropriate. Confirm to him, and to the class, that you are staying on track with the lesson plan. If the student continues to complain, remove him from the class and speak with him privately. More often than we teachers realize, our students' rudeness arises from personal problems that don't involve us at all.

Guideline #3: See the big picture

This guideline reminds teachers to use professional judgment to evaluate each situation as a unique moment, colored by various nuances.

Because teachers work with individual kids in specific circumstances, cookie-cutter punishments for certain behaviors aren't a solution. Jade's rude remark might be attributable to irritability brought on by hunger; Ramon's rude remark might simply be trying to make you mad. Although your initial response should look the same—you would, perhaps, remove both Jade and Ramon from the classroom and conduct a one-on-one conference in the hall—from then on, it's up to you to investigate the true source of the individual's behavior. This might be as simple as asking, "Are you OK? The remarks you made were unnecessary and hurtful. Is there something bugging you that I can help you with?" In other words, use your judgment to decide if the right response is punishment or a pack of crackers or just a little more time and attention. It shows you care. And your students will know it.

Guideline #4: Don't sell out your values

Each teacher has a set of personal values and brings those values into the classroom. Each teacher is challenged to honor those values amid the 10,000 or so practical challenges of the profession—teaching the curriculum, keeping order, addressing test scores, honoring faculty commitments, adhering to schoolwide objectives, and on and on—and if possible, communicate these values to students. This can be a tough and risky business.

Here are some of my guiding values: I believe that each person is a worthwhile individual; I value honesty; I value passion and flair. To "sell out" these values would be to write off Jake as a "bad kid" and a lost cause, not worth all the time it will take to reach him and help him learn; to pretend to students that I know more than I do; and to restrict students to a very regimented way of approaching a problem and thus save myself the effort required to evaluate truly original work and explore unorthodox points of view. Instead, I honor my values by not taking the easy way out: by managing my classroom in a manner that promotes individuality, honesty, passion, and flair; and by having my students read literature that addresses these themes.

What do you value? Recognize your values and then honor them by designing a classroom that reflects them.

• Maybe you value concern for others. Honor that value by organizing a charitable project: perhaps a "math-a-thon," where students raise money for a cause by getting pledges based on the number of math problems they will complete on a given day. A sellout would allow time constraints and the actual work required to dissuade him from doing this kind of project; he'd opt instead to address the concepts through another worksheet.

• Maybe you value teamwork. Teach these skills to your students by discussing the elements of teamwork and let them practice. A sellout might be put off by students' initial struggles with this complex kind of social interaction.

• Maybe you value beauty. Create an art contest where your students create a piece that answers the question, "What is beauty?" A sellout would be reluctant to decorate his classroom with beautiful things because he'd worry that students wouldn't appreciate them or would damage them.

It's true that honoring your values can be difficult. I decorated my first classroom with pictures of flowers, fish, panoramic views, and other beautiful things because I wanted my students to have something that might pique their interest if they faded away from my lesson. My principal commented, "Nice pictures," with disdain in her voice. (Looking back, I think she probably objected to the tape on the walls more than anything.) Well, I was tempted to sellout and remove the decorations for fear of irritating my principal. But I kept those pictures up, and I enjoyed the many conversations and essays that they inspired.

By figuring out what you value, you just might hit upon the reason an element of your teaching life isn't working. Share your values with your students by modeling them in your classroom. The more you do it, the more you will care about your classroom, your teaching life, and your students. And just maybe, reflecting on your values will remind you why you went into teaching in the first place.

The guidelines in action

I don't come right out and tell the kids these guidelines. I have found that people believe actions much more than they believe words.

Here's an illustration. Derrick was a student who was a pro at asking favors of me while I was in the middle of dealing with three other things. One morning, Derrick came running up with an emergency: "Coach Kelly needs to see me! It's important. I won't play tonight if I don't go now." Meanwhile, the bell's ringing, students are talking, the principal's making an announcement over the PA system, and another student is explaining to me why she does not have her homework.

How would you have handled this situation? It would be really tempting to just say, "Go." This would get the student out of your hair, but it would also put him in charge and leave you feeling manipulated. It might also mean that you'd have to deal with this maneuver all year long.

Instead of going that route—the easy way with hidden consequences—I looked to my guidelines. "Derrick," I said, "you will need to wait a minute until I have time to answer your question." *(Guideline #1: Don't let students fast-talk you.)* This let him know that I was following my preset class rules, not ignoring him, and he had no reason to get angry with me. It also gave me time to move beyond the overwhelmed feeling that creeps over me when I am blasted with so many stimuli at one time.

I began class with my usual steps, and when I had a moment, I went over to Derrick for a private chat. "Now I have time to hear you," I said. "Tell me what's going on."

"Like I said, I need to see Coach Kelly," he said impatiently.

"Did he give you a pass?" I asked. *(Guideline #2: Stay focused on the problem.)*

"No, but I can get one."

"Derrick, you know you can't leave class without a pass. I'm sorry, you can't go."

A week or so later, Derrick tried again. He arrived in class with word of another emergency meeting with Coach Kelly—right now!

Again, I acknowledged that I'd heard him, asked him to sit, began class, and then approached him privately.

"Did Coach Kelly give you a pass?"

"Yes, here it is," Derrick said, presenting a folded-up piece of notebook paper.

"This looks like your handwriting, Derrick. I'm not comfortable allowing you to go see Coach Kelly with this pass." *(Guideline #4: Don't sell out your values.)*

"But he wrote it."

"OK, for the sake of argument, let's say he wrote it. I'll keep this pass and write you another one. But after school, I will ask Coach Kelly if he wrote you this pass. If he did, no problem. If he didn't, you'll suffer the consequences, and that means you won't play tonight or maybe worse." *(Guideline #2: Stay focused on the problem. Guideline #3: See the big picture.)*

By being true to my own guidelines, I turned a frustrating situation into a well-reasoned one. I modeled calm, logical thinking focused on the student's need (to get out of class) and my need (to keep him in class). I gave Derrick a choice: He could say "forget it," and I would, or he could bluff and say, "OK, ask Coach yourself." I let him know where I stood and what the consequences would be. And I let him know that I would not offer those choices the next time a similar situation arose. There would be no surprises from or for anyone.

Chances are you have encountered a student accustomed to getting exactly what he wants because he can create and control chaos in the classroom. "Homework is for punks." "Why are you running to class?" These are comments a manipulator will make to teachers and other students. He places himself above the rules because the adults around him have allowed him to do this. When a student can manipulate his teacher, the teacher loses that student's respect; every grade, every lesson, and every comment become negotiable and up for the student's censure.

Teachers who allow this help to create a person who cannot work on teams, cannot manage his time or resources, and cannot feel satisfaction from earning something. Why earn a test grade when you can persuade the teacher to disregard the test? Why be on time when you can persuade another teacher to write you a pass? The student is cheated out of living within the world of reasonable expectations. And the teachers are cheating themselves as well, because instead of using their energy to recognize and respond responsibly to the student, they are wasting it after the fact on frustration, anger, and disdain.

When you first meet a manipulator, stick to the four guidelines. Do not allow time constraints, the student's rush-rush tone of voice, or any other factors to cause you to become caught up in the wave of confusion he is trying to generate. He will not be easily converted to your calm thinking, but stay the course. These difficult times will pay off as the manipulator learns to conform to the high expectations that you have set for him.

Classroom management is not about winning or losing; it's about having expectations of yourself and your students and standing by them for the betterment of everyone involved.

Caring Comes First

One sad thing about this world is that the acts that take the most out of you are usually the ones that other people will never know about.
—Anne Tyler

I spoke to a fellow English teacher about my philosophy of having to care about a student before you can teach him. "Oh, I tried that," she told me. "I told them I was there for them. I even let them goof around a little, but they never respected me. So I had to toughen up. Now I make sure to win every argument." She might be winning arguments, but she is losing a lot of ground. Her students disrespect her, they do not like themselves when they are in her class, and they are not learning very much about English literature.

Caring is a bridge to whatever a student defines as success. Frustration, hostility, confusion, and hatred are bridges to failure. When you are harboring a simmering rage, you cannot think effectively. If you are angry with a person, you are not able to handle that person effectively. Kelvin tested my ability to do both these things. He was an angry 16-year-old transfer student from New York, assigned to my freshman English class. How can I put this? Kelvin oozed evil. My first response to him was to ooze evil feelings right back, but then I listened to my heart. It said, "This kid is too old to be in this class. He doesn't want to be here." My evil feelings stopped. I smiled at Kelvin and his classmates, took attendance, and started the first day of class.

On the second day, Kelvin showed up wearing a hat, which is a violation of school rules. That's when our tradition started: "Good morning, Kelvin," I'd say. "Go ahead and lose the hat." He would grumble, but he would take it off. I find it's really difficult for a student to be hateful to someone who has said good morning to him. Kelvin was no different.

We got along for a while, but then he tested some of my class rules. Nobody is allowed to work on anything but the class assignment without my permission. While his classmates were working on a project about Icarus and Daedalus, Kelvin chose to write in his notebook. I went over to his desk and asked him if he needed any help starting on his project.

"Man, I'm not bothering anyone," he replied. "I'm just rappin'."

I said, "That would be fine if that were the assignment. I would like for you to do the assignment, so you can pass the class." *(Guideline #2: Stay focused on the problem.)*

"Man, leave me alone."

At this point, other students' ears were perking up around us, and the low buzz of working freshmen dulled to a lower buzz.

I asked Kelvin if I could speak with him in the hallway. *(Guideline #3: See the big picture. Guideline #4: Don't sell out your values.)* He did not answer, but he did get up and walk toward the door. I followed, telling the rest of the class that they were progressing nicely and should keep it up.

It would've been easy to get mad at this kid or send him to the office, but it wouldn't have solved anything. Instead, we talked. "Kelvin, my expectation is that you will do the work I assign unless there is a reason why you are unable to complete it," I explained. "Is there anything about this assignment that prevents you from starting it?" *(Guideline #2: Stay focused on the problem.)*

"No. Except that it's stupid," Kelvin said.

"You have a choice of three different types of projects," I pointed out. "If you don't like any of them, come up with an alternate and show it to me. If I feel it is challenging enough and meets my objective, I will approve it. Will that work?" *(Guideline #3: See the big picture.)*

"I'll see," he relented.

We went back into the classroom, and Kelvin took out his textbook and worked the rest of the period. I left him alone.

During my next planning period, I called Kelvin's uncle (who was his guardian) and expressed concern about Kelvin. I made sure to explain that I understood Kelvin was older than the other students in his class, and perhaps he found the 9th grade material boring. Nonetheless, I expected him to complete his assignments. The uncle thanked me for working with Kelvin instead of just kicking him out.

The next day, Kelvin asked me if he could speak to me out in the hallway. (He was following my modeling!) Once the rest of the class was started on their projects, we stepped out for a talk. "I don't appreciate you calling my uncle, telling him that I disrupted the class," Kelvin said.

Disrupted the class? I was floored. Had Kelvin's uncle misheard me? Had Kelvin misheard his uncle? "Kelvin, I told your uncle I was concerned about you not doing the class work. I will call him to clear up the confusion. It certainly was not my intention to get you in trouble." *(Guideline #4: Don't sell out your values.)*

"No, no, don't call," he demanded.

"Kelvin, I want my message to your uncle to be clearly heard," I explained. "And I do appreciate you keeping this matter private by asking me to speak to you in the hall. Let's go back in." *(Guideline #3: See the big picture.)*

I called the uncle, and sure enough, he had assumed that Kelvin had disturbed the class during his interaction with me. I explained that this wasn't so and told him that Kelvin had impressed me with how well he'd handled the situation. I also promised to call again when I had something positive to share about Kelvin.

I did not have to wait long. The next week, I called to report that Kelvin's participation in class had increased and that his level of anger toward me had dissipated. He and I had formed a person-to-person relationship. We both found a way to work comfortably with one another.

I am not going to lie and say that Kelvin became a model student or earned straight *As*. In fact, he passed just one quarter and had to repeat freshman English as a 17-year-old. But I am confident that he still came away with something tremendously important. In his closing letter to me, Kelvin wrote, "What I like about English is we talk about a lot of things. Most classes don't do that. We just get the work and do it and go to the next class. But in here we talk about the work and grades and what we need in class to pass." These comments told me that Kelvin and I had connected. My teaching style spoke to him. Although my bosses will never know this by the grades Kelvin received, Kelvin now knows that someone cares about whether he passes or fails, and also believes that he *can* pass. He can therefore believe it himself. Now he has a bridge to success, and he knows the choice is his. Will he walk across it or not?

"Acting out" is not the only way that students reach out. Some students will do everything you tell them to do, but if you listen closely, you can hear them calling out for attention, for an affirmation of their abilities, and for your love. Reginald was one such student. He was in my advanced junior English class, and his first words to me were "I'm not supposed to be in this class." He didn't believe he was good enough for advanced work.

I smiled and told him, "Well, I'm glad you're here, regardless." *(Guideline #4: Don't sell out your values.)*

Almost on a daily basis, Reginald would tell me that he didn't belong in advanced English. And whenever he did, I would respond by smiling at him, squeezing his shoulder, or just saying, "But I'm glad you're here." Eventually, Reginald confessed that he was not a good reader, and we worked out a plan where I would give him the reading assignments one day in advance. *(Guideline #2: Stay focused on the problem.)* He read in class, and slowly but surely, settled into the routine of a course that expected more of him than his "regular" courses did.

Reginald worked really hard all year. His writing progressed, he read John Steinbeck and Toni Morrison, and he gave a wonderful speech to the class. He even earned an *A* one quarter. He *was* an advanced student. The joke of him "not belonging in this class" truly became a joke—one that the entire class appreciated. He wrote me the following letter at the end of the school year, and it's one that makes me smile and cry at the same time.

> Dear Ms. Ridnouer,
>
> Your class has been the greatest learning experience that I have ever had. I really didn't like the reading assignments that we had but I am glad that I did them because I learned a lot. To be honest, there is nothing you can do to become a better teacher. You are the best. If you can take a child that has never been to an advanced class before and he takes it and makes his first *A* in a core class, you can feel good about yourself. Even though I act the way I do and never took the time to say that I thank you for all that you have done. I learned a lot in your class but you taught me more about myself. Now I realize that I just didn't believe in myself but now I know thanks to you.
>
> Love,
> Reginald
>
> P.S. Save this letter so when I make it big in track you can say, "I taught him about himself."

Students' Anger Isn't Necessarily About You

> *What lies behind us and what lies before us are tiny matters, compared to what lies within us.*
>
> —Ralph Waldo Emerson

In any given encounter with a student, it is easy for a teacher to assume that the emotions the student is expressing are directly related to that encounter. But this assumes that students are in control of their emotions and are logically relaying these emotions to the party who gave rise to them. And that assumption belies the fact that students are still maturing. I am not saying that students should not be held responsible for their own behavior. What I am saying is that if a student does display anger, realize that it might not be about you.

The kids we teach have a lot going on. Consider that they have parents, other family, friends, a bus driver, a principal, seven or eight teachers, various coaches, and maybe even a boss who all feel justified in telling them how to behave. Consider that all this is compounded with realities like divorce, violence, and peer, social, and economic pressures. A student might have a difficult time responding calmly to one more person telling him to take off his hat. What's essential is that we, as teachers, exhibit the maturity that our students have not yet attained. The four guidelines are extremely helpful here in that they provide a way to maintain control over ourselves rather than allow others to control us.

My students and I talk about this idea of control in relationship to literature as we study the philosophies of determinism and transcendentalism. Determinism is the belief that a person's life is not under his own command; each decision he makes is really a response to elements that he cannot control. Transcendentalism is the belief that a person can move beyond the boundaries set by society and is then free to define himself in his own terms. The overwhelming majority of my students are attracted to transcendentalism, and yet, they exhibit determinist behaviors. For example, they say that they would punch a person who said something bad about their mother, even if that would mean being suspended. They also say they believe that their skin color limits their career choices. They allow their decisions not only to be *influenced* by outside forces but to be *controlled* by them.

My students are always a little surprised to realize the difference between a philosophy they like and the actual philosophy that they ascribe to. After some discussion, some of them admit that maybe they *could* control their own lives. It's a powerful lesson; I can see the students integrating the class work into their own lives and positively changing themselves.

Learn to Hold Your Tongue

It's so easy to be wicked without knowing it, isn't it?
—L. M. Montgomery

It's really easy to jump on every little infraction with a harsh word; it's much more challenging to give a student time and space to correct the behavior. Of course, this doesn't mean you stand back and watch students fight, hoping they will stop eventually. But what about that chatty little student, or the sleepy one? A few looks and a few shoulder squeezes are very effective and do not cause the negative emotions that a "Shhh!" or a "Sit up!" triggers.

Sometimes other students will intervene and relieve you of some of the burden of classroom management. It's always nice to have a kid in class who is a natural leader and also on your side. With a little encouragement, that kid is likely to accept a leadership role in quieting the class or insisting that other students be respectful. Often, a few words from this peer can be more effective than any directions, corrections, or encouragement you can give.

I think of Amadeo, an outgoing, silly kid whose silliness other students responded to in a positive way. One day, Debbie fell asleep while we were reading *A Raisin in the Sun* aloud. When she was startled awake after missing a line, she had a difficult time getting started again; she mumbled and sounded nothing like the dignified "Mama" she had portrayed the day before. After Debbie haltingly read a few lines, Amadeo called out, "Hey, what's wrong with Mama?" Everyone laughed, including me. It was just the right thing to break the tension and get Mama back on track.

Your Words Matter

Where so many hours have been spent in convincing myself that I am right, is there not some reason to fear I may be wrong?
—Jane Austen

There is no such thing as a casual remark to a student. We all know that students can tune teachers out, but we sometimes forget that they can *tune us in* to the same degree. An offhand remark might echo for years. This can be a negative thing, like when we let our tongue slip ahead of both our brain and our heart and tell a student that she is stupid. But it can be positive too, like when we tell a student that she is a good writer.

I have seen for myself how positive offhand comments can take root and really help. This was the case with Latrice, who was 16 years old and repeating 9th grade English. She rarely came to class, and by the end of the first semester, she had gotten pregnant, had had a miscarriage, and was failing all her classes. I had tried talking to Latrice privately and I'd tried calling her home, but she was still failing. During my planning period one day, I saw her at the pay phone when she should have been in class. I asked her why she was wasting her time roaming the halls and talking on the phone.

She started to explain: "Wasting time? No, really, I . . . ." She stopped.

"Latrice, you're a smart young lady," I said. "Don't give up on you. I haven't. Come to class and do the work. You'll pass. I promise." This is something I say to one student or another probably twice a week. I did not give the conversation another thought.

Well, Latrice started coming to class every day with completed homework and a willing spirit, and this behavior continued for the rest of the year. The only recognition I gave her were smiles; the passing grades, she earned herself. Then, on the last day of school, Latrice stopped in to see me, and I could see she had something important to say. She looked serious. She looked confident.

"Ms. Ridnouer, I want to thank you for telling me I could pass in school when nobody else would. Because you told me that, I worked hard in your class and in all my classes. Thank you."

My eyes began to well with tears. I tried to tell Latrice that she was worth my time and reiterate that I believed in her, but she hadn't come for a conversation. She had said what she'd come to say, and now she was ready to move on. So I told her that I hoped she would have a good summer, and then she was gone. I just sat at my desk and glowed for a minute—alone, but surrounded with images of students like Latrice, Reginald, and Kelvin.

Every Interaction Is an Opportunity to Learn

Every spirit builds itself a house, and beyond its house a world, and beyond its world a heaven. Know then that the world exists for you.

—Ralph Waldo Emerson

It takes time and care to teach students to think—to not just accept what they're told but to do the research, consult other points of view, ask questions, form their own conclusions, and defend those conclusions with a reasoned argument. I do this by admitting when I must struggle to find an explanation for some element of a reading and by modeling the thinking process. I also decline to serve as The Great Answerer of All Questions, who is always ready to tell students what is right or true. I meet their questions with questions of my own and encourage them to form their own opinions and to be ready to defend them. As they gain confidence with this process, some begin challenging people who had gone unchallenged before. Some of these people are their other teachers, and a few of them become upset and say, "You cannot question me like that!" The fact of the matter is they can, and they do. As teachers, we can choose to shut down and be defensive about a lesson, or choose to support an honest expression of student opinion and learn what our students are really trying to say.

A defensive dialogue might go like this:

Eric:　　　　Ms. Haverly, putting the play on was a stupid idea.
Ms. Haverly: You can't talk to me like that!

Eric: Watch me.

Ms. Haverly: Watch *me* kick your butt right out of this classroom.

In this exchange, Ms. Haverly strays from guidelines #2 *(stay focused on the problem)* and #4 *(don't sell out your values)*. The message she's sending to her students is that perhaps the lesson *was* stupid and that she is the kind of teacher who will waste time arguing and threatening a student.

It's possible to direct the kind of discussion that will support your lesson and still allow students to express opinions in a constructive way. A supportive dialogue might go like this:

Eric: Ms. Haverly, putting the play on was a stupid idea.

Ms. Haverly: What kind of skills do you think I'm trying to teach by having you put on the play? *(Guideline #1: Don't let students fast-talk you. Guideline #3: See the big picture.)*

Eric: How to bore us.

Ms. Haverly: No, really. Does anyone have an opinion? *(Guideline #2: Stay focused on the problem. Guideline #3: See the big picture.)*

Danielle: It helps us understand stage directions and dialogue.

Ms. Haverly: Good! What else?

Stephanie: Well, we have to speak in front of the whole class. . . .

Ms. Haverly: Yes! What else?

Deron: I've never read anything as many times as I've read this play.

Ms. Haverly: And how do you feel about that?

Deron: I know I understand the smaller points that I missed the first time we read this.

Ms. Haverly: So this is helping our reading comprehension?

Jamel: Yeah. And what about cooperation? We're learning to help each other stay on cue and to read lines effectively.

Ms. Haverly: You guys are right on target. *(Guideline #4: Don't sell out your values.)*

Eric: OK, maybe it's not stupid. But I hate my part.

Now the truth comes out. Instead of kicking Eric out of class for being rude, his teacher helps him articulate the real problem he is having so that they may solve it. Another student volunteers to swap parts, and the matter is settled.

Although it's time-consuming, the kind of back-and-forth questioning illustrated in this scenario accomplishes many things. The teacher not only resolves a potential discipline concern but also sends the message that she cares about the students' opinions. She shows them how much they already know and solidifies the group's commitment to the assignment. She models how to redirect a potential conflict, and she keeps the focus on the day's lesson. Students feel that she cares.

Questions for Reflection

1. What is your definition of a "good" teacher?

2. Do you share personal information with students to help them see you as a real person?

3. How might the four guidelines improve your teaching day? Is there one guideline you think might be particularly helpful?

4. What do you value? How might you alter your classroom management practices to honor your values more explicitly? How might you integrate the teaching of these values into your lesson planning?

5. What are some behaviors students might display to cover up a learning disability, discomfort with a subject, or an outside problem?

6. How do you respond to these problems?

7. What are some opportunities for teaching that you have missed during interactions with students? What would you do during these teachable moments now?

8. Who encouraged you to develop your voice? How have you adapted this person's method for use in your own classroom?

3

Balancing Care and Discipline

Living is a form of not being sure, not knowing what's next or how. The moment you know how, you begin to die a little. The artist never entirely knows. We guess. We may be wrong, but we take leap after leap in the dark.

—Agnes de Mille

Teaching is a high-wire act that must be practiced every day. We show our care for students through high expectations, awareness of their lives, and being human with them. Some days this is easy; other days it is not. One day a polite student will suddenly be rude. Find out why, privately and respectfully. Do not assume to know why a student is behaving poorly; make the leap to hear his response. Plan responses that will help you maintain your professionalism and respect each student's needs.

Another student stops coming to class because, as she tells you in the hallway, "I'm flunking anyway. So why bother?" It's a fair question. Call the student's home. Offer tutoring. Encourage her to come to class. Follow the disciplinary measures your school has designed.

Do not take it as a personal affront; do not ignore or nag her. If you do, she will use your reaction as an excuse for her failure instead of trying to make a change for the better.

One year I had two students, both juniors, who just decided to stop coming to class. I used the tactics I've just described. I told both of them that they could make up the work. I talked to their parents. I told them every time that I saw them that I missed them and would love to help them. I wrote referrals to the office, and the administration disciplined them.

The result? One student began coming to class again; the other did not. The one who did, Megan, came to me at the end of the year to tell me "something very serious." She said, "Ms. Ridnouer, you believed in me and kept encouraging me when nobody else did. Because of you, I believed in myself, passed your class, and did better in all of my classes. Thank you." Lauren, who did not return to class, chose to fail, but she still turned in her textbook to me with a smile on her face. I hope she will turn that smile inward on herself and believe that she can pass junior English.

Ralph Waldo Emerson was right when he said that "the secret to education lies in respecting the pupil." I respected Lauren as an individual, and she responded as an individual, which turned out not to be exactly the way I wanted her to respond. *(Guideline #2: Stay focused on the problem. Guideline #4: Don't sell out your values.)* No, she didn't learn all the material in the curriculum, but she did learn how to handle a problem without being rude or intolerant. If you treat each student as a unique individual with a life separate from your own experience, you will connect with that student or end the school year trying. That's all you can do.

Getting Past Personality Conflicts

The life which is not examined is not worth living.

—Plato

Have you ever had a student who pushed every one of your buttons? My "buttons" include know-it-all people, rude people, and argumentative, illogical people. Cecilia had all of these traits and displayed them fairly consistently. She was also an extremely bright girl who excelled in class work, but she struggled to complete tasks that required her attention over an extended period of time.

I allowed Cecilia to push my buttons, and, as a result, I let myself be angry and irrational toward her and the rest of the class. I was not respecting the dignity of Cecilia, her classmates, or myself. And I let myself stray from one of the most important pieces of advice I've ever received from a student: to never "turn" on the entire class out of exasperation with one disruptive student.

When I finally realized what was happening, I did many things. I revamped the seating chart, putting Cecilia in the front and center of the classroom. I talked to the students about my frustrations in working with the class, not mentioning Cecilia specifically. I also began ignoring her interruptions and insisting that she respond only when I asked everyone else to respond. *(Guideline #2: Stay focused on the problem.)* And I refused to listen to her flimsy arguments about late assignments and excuse notes. *(Guideline #1: Don't let students fast-talk you.)* Basically, I stopped allowing my annoyance with Cecilia's behavior to give her an avenue to escape responsibility for it. *(Guideline #4: Don't sell out your values.)*

The class took note, and they began ignoring Cecilia's rude comments too. They also seemed to focus more on the academics of the class instead of its internal chemistry. I began to see qualities in some of my other students that I hadn't had time to notice when I was allowing Cecilia to monopolize my attention.

What about Cecilia? How did she fare in all of this? Well, she began saying "I'm sorry" when she interrupted me and the other students, and as the days went on, she interrupted less often. She started showing up to class on time. Yes, she remained opinionated, but she no longer dominated class discussions. I left the door wide open for her to share her opinions, but her classmates and I stopped taking up her invitations to argue. The guidelines worked.

Creating Boundaries

It is in the knowledge of the genuine conditions of our lives that we must draw our strength to live and our reasons for living.
—Simone de Beauvoir

Kids of all ages want boundaries. Think of the classroom as a soccer field. There are distinct lines demarcating both the "in" zones and the "out" zones. The players know when the ball is in play or out of play, and the spectators do too.

Of course, the reality is not quite so simple. The boundaries some teachers set are acceptable to the students, and they manage to stay within them rather easily. The boundaries other teachers set are unacceptable, and students find themselves straying out of bounds and constantly receiving negative responses from these teachers. If a teacher's response to a student's behavior is erratic, the student does not know from one day to the next if the teacher considers this student a "good" or a "bad" kid. This may seem trivial, but students paint themselves in the broad stripes of black or white, bad or good, and they assume that teachers see them the same way. When they cannot pinpoint exactly how you feel about them, they often decide that you think of them negatively, and they behave negatively in turn.

At the very beginning of the school year, let your students know where you draw the lines in your classroom and what constitutes behavior that is out of bounds. Set these boundaries according to your student population and your own comfort levels, and make sure the rules are clear. The message that students must receive is that you want a calm and orderly classroom and you will work hard to maintain it. Explain that your rules are there to help them choose their own behavior.

Students who choose to stay in the "in" zone by following the rules, being cooperative, and attending class every day could be doing it for any number of reasons, including habit and a desire to please you or their parents. Those who choose to enter the "out" zone by misbehaving, failing to do work, and arriving late to class could be making this choice for myriad reasons as well: They want attention, they are bored or frustrated, they are suffering some sort of abuse, or other reasons. Each student's choice sends a message that you should be receiving and responding to, especially the "out" zone choices.

As teachers, it's our responsibility to receive these messages, and classroom management is what makes this possible. In a chaotic classroom where rules change every day, it is difficult to know whether a student's rude remarks are due to the classroom environment or if there are other problems in her life that she is trying to relay. But if the rules are set, discussed, posted, and enforced consistently, you have a better chance of picking up the real meaning of what a student is saying instead of getting lost in the emotive aspects of her words. For example, should a student tell you that you chose to assign *Huckleberry Finn* because you are a racist who thinks blacks can only speak like stupid people, instead of being shocked into silence, you'll be able to talk to her about the issue. You can be certain that she has problems in her life that do not involve you, and she wants you to help her resolve them. She is asking for help the only way that many teenagers know how.

A calm classroom environment eliminates possibly distracting stimuli. This reduces the chance of poor behavior because the students feel more comfortable and can more readily choose to follow your directions and focus on the learning at hand. As teachers, we cannot control our students' behavior, but we can help delineate the behavioral choices they will feel good about making.

A Four-Step Process for Caring Discipline

I merely took the energy it takes to pout and wrote some blues.
—Duke Ellington

Teachers should never make idle threats. Telling a student, "I am going to send you to the principal's office if you do that one more time," does not generally change student behavior unless you intend to keep your eyes solely on that one child for the rest of the period. When a disciplinary situation arises, I follow a four-step process, which I've found to be a more effective use of my energy. It not only reduces whole-class involvement in incidents or altercations, it models the cool-as-a-cucumber behavior that students need to incorporate into their own lives, so they can build and maintain relationships throughout their lives.

Step 1: A nonverbal warning

When you notice someone whose behavior is off task or otherwise out of bounds, take a private, mostly nonverbal approach. Make eye contact, squeeze the student's shoulder, or lean down and whisper, "May I help you with something?"

These are all nonpunitive approaches that tell the student you're aware of what's going on and you would like it to stop. *(Guideline #3: See the big picture.)* Posing the question ("May I help you with something?") also acknowledges the student might be engaging in the out-of-bounds behavior because of confusion about the assignment. *(Guideline #2: Stay focused on the problem.)* All of these caring, low-key, direct-contact approaches respect the student and give him a reason to simply stop doing what he is doing. It removes the chance of angering, shaming, or frustrating the child. The reverse tactic— yelling at the student to be quiet or sit down or sit up—gives him, and possibly the entire class, someone to respond to negatively.

Step 2: A verbal warning

If the student persists, quietly inform him that you will need to see him after class. This gives the student time to think about his actions and stop them, showing you that he is capable of working within your limits. It also tells the rest of the class that you are aware of the problem and will handle it. *(Guideline #4: Don't sell out your values.)*

When speaking to the student after class, ask him to explain why he was misbehaving and then listen closely to what he has to say. Let him talk without judging him, shaming him, or making excuses for him. Your role is to be a sounding board for how that student can stop the behavior.

Step 3: A private conversation

If the behavior persists or reoccurs during the same class period, figure out a way to have a private talk with the student right then. I usually meet with the student in the hallway. Of course, this can be frustrating if you are lecturing, for example, or conducting another activity that you must lead. (I keep an alternative assignment at the ready for just this kind of situation.) The temptation is certainly to send the student out or to ignore the behavior. Each teacher's decision here will be based on his or her level of tolerance and the kind of classroom atmosphere that's most conducive to the particular group of students' learning. *(Guideline #3: See the big picture.)* To me, sending the student out often feels as though I am giving up too soon. Ignoring the behavior reduces the lesson's effectiveness and sends the message that it's OK to disrupt class.

When you confer with a disruptive student during class, be brief. Most people quit listening after about 30 seconds of lecture, so it's essential to take advantage of this small window of time and get that student's attention. Use "I" messages: *"I am trying to teach the class, but your constant disruptions are slowing me down. This frustrates me." "I sense that you are having trouble settling in today."* Let the student respond from there. By not judging the student for his particular behavior, you open the door for an honest response that is more likely to lead to the problem's resolution.

Step 4: Removal from class and a conversation with parents

If the behavior persists, have the student removed from class. It is unfair to allow one person to dominate the class and cheat the other students out of their education. In our school, we have "lockout." This is a monitored room where teachers send all tardy students and students who are causing disciplinary problems.

Whenever I must remove a student from class, I contact his or her parents that evening and explain the situation. I've learned that when speaking with a parent, it's helpful to continue the use of "I" messages: *"I am concerned about your son's ability to achieve in my class. I hope that together we can come up with a strategy for success."* Make sure to have other pertinent information, such as the student's grades and attendance records, at your fingertips so that you will be able to give a full account of the student's situation and answer the parent's questions.

This four-step approach can work for every teacher. I find that it helps me achieve many positive emotional outcomes for the misbehaving student and also for myself and the rest of the class. The student comes away with a renewed awareness of behavioral expectations and a sense that I care about him as much as I care about my own personal need to teach the lesson. The rest of the class sees that their teacher respects students too much to embarrass them in front of their peers. They also see that misbehaving students will have chances to improve their behavior before suffering serious consequences. Of course, I win because, ultimately, I am able to resume my lesson plan and maintain a good relationship with my students.

Choosing Your Battles

There is no duty we so much underrate as the duty of being happy.
By being happy we sow anonymous benefits upon the world.
—Robert Louis Stevenson

Think about all the rules that govern student behavior. Some are set up for simple safety reasons; "no hitting" comes quickly to mind. But there are other rules with rationales that are not so clear, and if a teacher doesn't agree that these rules are necessary, that teacher is likely to be lax about enforcing them. A school might have 150 staff members, and with so many personalities scrutinizing each rule, varying interpretations and degrees of enforcement are to be expected.

Personally, I lump rules into two categories: rules that promote learning and rules that do not affect learning. A rule prohibiting tardiness is a good example of the first category. If students are allowed to simply trickle in, there's no definite beginning of the class, and this slows everyone down. In addition, we only have 48 minutes in a class period and I value every second as if it were gold. However, I once worked with a teacher who didn't share this outlook. Not only did she allow tardy students into her classroom without consequences, but she would write passes for students she didn't teach to excuse tardies to another teacher's class. To my mind, this policy taught the kids that for every rule, there is someone who will help you get around it.

I spent some time being frustrated over how this teacher was shortchanging her students (and mine!) when she wrote these illegitimate passes. Then I remembered the famous prayer by Reinhold Niebuhr that my grandmother had hanging in her kitchen: "God, grant me the serenity to accept the things I cannot change, the courage to change the things I can, and the wisdom to know the difference." I was in no position to tell another teacher how to conduct herself professionally. My challenge was to change the things I could change: how I ran my own classroom. I did this by telling my students that I would only accept passes from an administrator or their previous class's teacher. Since the illegitimate pass-writer taught the same grade and subject that I did, none of my students would ever find themselves in a position to get a legitimate pass from her.

At my school, when students are tardy without a pass, they must go to lockout and stay there for the entire period. They earn an unexcused absence, but they can make up the class work. I don't like my students to miss classroom time, but I stay firm on this rule to show that I value *everyone's* time. *(Guideline #4: Don't sell out your values.)* Even though it was hard to send a conscientious student like Lassandra to lockout when she was two minutes late, I did it. The rest of the class saw it, she saw it, and no one had a reason to question whether tardiness was a rule that I enforced.

Now, to the second category of rules: the kind that have no effect on learning. A perfect example is a rule prohibiting chewing gum—

something that does not interfere with the educational process provided that students don't blow bubbles or chomp like mad dogs. It is also a rule that's difficult to monitor and enforce, as students can swallow the evidence and then put in a new piece five minutes later.

When I first began teaching, if I saw a student chewing gum, I would either bring over the garbage can or ask the student to get up and go spit out the gum. It took time away from my lesson, made the gum-chewer mad, and gave everyone else an opportunity to ask me why that rule was in place. I would invite students who asked me that question to stay after class to discuss the issue, at which time I would dutifully explain the policy. After a few of these after-class sessions, I realized I did not really care about gum chewing. I began asking students to spit out gum only if they were snapping it or blowing bubbles or otherwise distracting their classmates. *(Guideline #3: See the big picture.)* I did not tell the students about my decision; I just changed my reaction. It was never a problem after that.

I did have one student who seemed to get so lost in her work that she would start smacking and cracking her gum. When this happened, the entire class would let her know that this was unacceptable ("*Gross,* Demetria!"). She stopped, and I never had to say a word. Sometimes peer pressure can be a teacher's friend.

Referrals to the Office

Things do not change; we change.
—Henry David Thoreau

Many teachers rely on referrals to administrators to handle their discipline problems. Basically, these teachers are passing their responsibility for particular students to someone who has the power to remove the student from class for a few days. I am not saying there isn't a time and a place for referrals, but in my experience, consistently following the four guidelines allows teachers to solve most discipline problems on their own, without involving the administration. Students who do not respond to this approach need the attention of somebody besides a classroom teacher.

What about serious problems you might encounter outside the classroom—say, in the hallway or the cafeteria? There the standard for a referral might be a little lower. If I must intervene in incidents involving students I do not teach, I still attempt to follow the four guidelines; however, because I will not have the time to work with these kids or influence their behavior on a regular basis, I am quicker to write up referrals to the office. An administrator needs to get involved.

Some administrators are better than others at supporting teachers' disciplinary actions. Some won't support you at all, and although they probably won't come and tell you this, you'll get the message when your referrals are ignored or misplaced. I was in this situation once, and even after I spoke privately to the administrator about a lack of support, I saw no change. Remembering the Serenity Prayer, I decided to keep writing the referrals to this administrator, although I no longer expected a response. With each referral I wrote, I reminded this person that I was doing my job while he was not.

Speaking of which: Always keep a copy of every referral or other discipline documentation that you submit. Paperwork has a way of "walking away" in a busy school office. File your copy in a place where you can locate it quickly in case follow-up is necessary. It's also wise to document parent phone calls. Write down the dates you called and whether or not you made contact. If you keep this up to date, nobody can accuse you of failing to do your job.

Invariably, you will have students who need ongoing reminders of your policies. I recommend maintaining individual documentation folders for these students. And if you have students who are continually disruptive, keep individual journals documenting their behavior: simple descriptions of the student's actions and the dates they occurred. Make sure to include the good and the bad; when it comes time for the administration or student services to take action, you want them to be able to read this journal without thinking you have a certain bias against the student. Is maintaining a behavior journal on a student a sign that you "have it out" for that child? Quite the contrary: It's a sign of professional concern and says loud and clear, "I care about this child. Here is the pattern of behavior that needs immediate attention."

Helping a Student Change His or Her Behavior

No pessimist ever discovered the secrets of the stars, or sailed to an uncharted land, or opened a new heaven to the human spirit.
—Helen Keller

Adolescent students like to be authorities over their own behavior, and they behave or misbehave to send whatever message they feel like sending at that moment. This message could come in the form of shooting spitballs at a classmate, talking back, sleeping at their desk, or staring out the window. If you have taken the time and care to develop a positive relationship with your students, they will usually change their behavior when you point out its negative impact on the class. In contrast, a teacher who relies on commands to change a student's behavior ("That's enough!" "Wake up, and sit up straight." "Eyes on me, please!") has nothing but those commands to rely on; the "corrected" student is likely to modify the behavior only temporarily, if at all.

I've experienced this with students whom I don't know. For example, my school has a rule of no hats in the hallway, and most students adhere to it. Occasionally, while standing outside my classroom between classes, I'll spot a hat wearer and have to say, "Sir, lose the hat." Some of these students take off their hats with an "Oops, my bad," and others just take off their hats without comment. They might put those hats on again after turning the corner—I just don't know. But there are a few students who look back defiantly and ignore my command. This forces me into a decision: Ignore the child's defiance or uphold the rule? Nine times out of 10, I uphold the rule and follow the student until he removes his hat. It's difficult to turn my back on a child who is so obviously looking for attention.

With our own students, whom we see every day, we can focus on helping them change their behavior for themselves and reinforce our guidance with words and action. I had the opportunity to do this with Monty. He was a gem of a student who worked diligently and cooperated well in my class. I saw him in the hall one day during my planning period. He didn't have a pass. I knew what that meant: He was on his way to lockout.

I stopped him and asked, "Hey, Monty, how are you doing?"

"Not so great," he replied. He knew that *I* knew where he was headed.

"What happened?"

"That Ms. Smith, she just threw me out of class for talking," he said.

"Sounds like she runs a pretty tight ship."

"Yeah. I was just telling this girl what the assignment was. I wasn't being loud."

"Hmm . . . I can see where this could be frustrating. What can you do to make sure you aren't put in this situation again?"

"Just tell the girl to ask the teacher what the assignment is?"

"Sounds good, but Ms. Smith might still get mad because you are still talking."

"Yeah. I don't know, then."

"What about body language?"

"You mean like pointing?"

"Yes."

"I guess I could just point to the teacher or point to the page number in my book to show her where we are."

"Sounds like you've come up with a good solution, Monty. I'll see you tomorrow in class."

It took Monty a few tries to perfect his idea, but he soon learned how to get along in Ms. Smith's class. Yes, he still thought she was being unreasonable, but he came to see that it was in his best interest to cooperate. The other options were to fail, become a discipline problem, or be switched into another class where he might meet another teacher just like Ms. Smith. Realizing when to go along to get along and knowing how to do this are real-world skills that Monty will be using for the rest of his life: not only in school but also at home, at work, and at social gatherings.

In-School Suspension

Work is love made visible.

—Kahlil Gibran

When one of my students is in in-school suspension (ISS), I hand-deliver the assignment and necessary materials to the student myself. I enter the ISS room, say good morning, and explain the assignment. I do not gripe at the student for getting into trouble. I prompt the student for questions, mention that I look forward to seeing him or her back in class, and then say goodbye.

A personal appearance in ISS sends many messages. It tells my students that I care enough to walk all the way down to the ISS room instead of simply putting the assignment in the much-closer monitor's box. It also tells them that I do not want them to fall behind, and that I understand that they somehow got into trouble but it does not matter to me. I just want them back in class.

I have been surprised to see that many students who usually do nothing in the classroom will do beautiful work in ISS. I do not know if it's because the assignment was handwritten and delivered just for them, or if they are simply doing good work to kill time. Whatever the reason, I will take it.

Finding Solutions and Making Mistakes

Perfectionism is the voice of the oppressor, the enemy of the people. It will keep you cramped and insane your whole life.

—Anne Lamott

Teaching many kids over the years is no guarantee that a teacher will know the perfect way to work with any particular kid. I believe that categorizing students into types—the good kids, the trouble-makers, the shy ones, and so on—is inherently dangerous: a box that restricts the kinds of approaches teachers take. Of course, categorizing a student is not the same as looking for a behavioral pattern that can help clarify the student's circumstances. Putting a student in a category predetermines the response you will give him. If you categorize him as a troublemaker, you are less likely to reason with him individually and more likely to send him to the office. However, looking for behavioral patterns is a way to connect individual students to students you've taught before, and you can use past responses as a starting point. If what worked before is not successful, you're free to modify the approach. The clarity you've gained on the current student's circumstances puts you one step closer to an individual solution that will work.

It's OK to make a mistake, because you will. In fact, I've found that students really appreciate it when a teacher admits to making a mistake. We impress them more when we say, "I don't know the answer to this problem," or "I messed up," than when we fake infal-libility. I had to own up to a mistake the day my students were finish-ing up a project on *Romeo and Juliet.* We had spent many days on this project, and nearing the end, all of us were eager to finish it. On the day before the projects were due, I told the students to get out their project materials while I took attendance and did a book check. Several voices called out with comments like, "Oh, I left my stuff at home," and "Can I have another assignment sheet?"

I ignored these comments and continued taking attendance. Then I got everyone's attention and asked, "Who needs another assignment sheet?" I passed them out along with the necessary books. "Are there any questions about the project? It is due tomorrow when you walk into class."

Mark raised his hand and said, "I need to go to my locker."

"I'm sorry, Mark," I responded. "You'll have to work on another aspect of your project. I don't allow students to go to their lockers during class."

Other kids chimed in with similar difficulties. I was becoming annoyed. Then Kelvin said, "Man, I've *got* to go to my locker."

That was it.

"Kelvin, you should've thought about that before you came to class!" I said in a nasty tone of voice.

"You don't have to yell at me," he replied. "I just made a simple mistake."

He was right. I needed to take a few breaths before I could talk to him about it. After quieting the class, I walked over to Kelvin, squeezed his shoulder, and said, "I'm sorry I yelled at you. I was getting really frustrated."

That was all I said. Somehow that was enough, and Kelvin found some project-related work to do. This gave me the energy to go deal with Mark, who was still not working on anything. He was a master at finding ways to get out of class, but with my renewed energy, we figured out a short assignment he could complete before the bell.

Sure, I had to lose a little face when I apologized to Kelvin, but I gained a lot of respect from him at the same time. I showed him that I make grievous errors in judgment too and that I need forgiveness for making these errors. As teachers, we expect students to apologize all the time, yet we seldom model the behavior ourselves. That should change.

Questions for Reflection

1. What are your "buttons"?

2. What can you do to prevent your students from pushing your buttons?

3. What is your method for evaluating your school day, week, or semester?

4. What steps do you take to address poor student behavior?

5. What battles do you avoid? Why?

6. What do you do when you see students who are in trouble?

7. Think of a time someone sincerely apologized to you. How did that affect you?

4

Handling Common Challenges

Do not weep; do not wax indignant. Understand.
—Baruch Spinoza

Although high schools are filled with incredibly diverse students, the behaviors these students exhibit—and the resulting challenges for teachers—can be strikingly similar. Awareness is the first step in handling these challenges and keeping learning on track. In this chapter, we'll look at some of the common problematic issues that teachers encounter, and I'll share some of the ways that I've thwarted their domination in my classroom. Again, at the root of my dealings with students is concern for a particular student's welfare while maintaining a calm, educational environment for the class as a whole.

Hallway Noise and Conflict

Opportunity just exists in the air for a few minutes. If you don't obey your gut feeling right away, you've lost your chance.
—Ken Hakuta

High school hallways tend to be noisy, chaotic places. One reason is that high school *students* are noisy. They like to speak over one another, and they tend not to interact in the most courteous of ways.

In my school, a student overhearing a hallway conversation and sharing an unsolicited comment might get a rude rebuke ("*You* are not in this conversation.") At first, I attempted to intervene in these sorts of situations ("Is that any way to talk? Come on, now, she's not trying to start trouble."). Now I see it as students' way of drawing boundaries. This may seem as if I am ducking my responsibility to help these students become responsible adults, but after observing many of these "rude" exchanges, I can see that they are relatively harmless. Fights are not started; feelings do not appear hurt. The "interrupters" simply make a mental note about the situation and move on. If they have enjoyed the attention, they will interrupt the same people again the next day. If the situation has embarrassed them, they will ignore the people the next day. My involvement would just make them mad, give all involved a common enemy, and make it impossible for them to learn any lesson from the situation. One of the most challenging aspects of monitoring student behavior is learning when to effectively interject your authority and when to simply butt out.

Teacher presence is the simplest way to reduce both the noise that leads to headaches and the tension that can lead to confrontation. I stand outside my door between classes: to greet each of my kids, to greet those kids who've become familiar faces, and to help keep the hall peaceful. A teacher's presence can stop a kid from running, fighting, picking on another kid, and engaging in other negative or destructive behaviors.

If you're like me, you've probably known teachers who stand outside their classroom, perhaps reading a memo or student essays, and remain oblivious to fights and all sorts of other infractions. When an administrator asks why an incident happened, they get defensive: "I was standing by my door. What else can I do?"

With that defeatist attitude, not much. But with a more proactive one, an individual teacher can accomplish a lot. Look up and down the hall. Smile and say "Good morning" or "Good afternoon." Look the poorly behaved students in the eye and keep a straight face; they will usually smile back. Most students do not want to get in trouble, but when you're faced with those few who do, don't be afraid to address them directly or call security. Individual students do not have the right to tyrannize an entire hallway.

Too often adolescents lose all sense of their true selves when the alternative is losing face in front of their peers. When intervening with individuals, try to bring them to a private place— perhaps around a corner or inside your classroom—so that they can truly be themselves. Then discuss the misbehavior in a calm way, perhaps as follows:

Teacher: Thank you for being cooperative and coming in here. *(Guideline #4: Don't sell out your values.)* I would appreciate it if you would keep your hands off other students in the hall. *(Guideline #2: Stay focused on the problem.)*

Student: But that girl likes it when I grab her!

Teacher: Whether she likes it or not doesn't matter. It's inappropriate to touch people like that at school. *(Guideline #2: Stay focused on the problem.)* Is this acceptable to you? *(Guideline #4: Don't sell out your values.)*

Student: Yeah, I guess it's OK.

Teacher: What can I expect to see tomorrow when you walk down the hall and see this girl? *(Guideline #2: Stay focused on the problem.)*

Student: I'll just say "Hey" or something like that.

Teacher: Great. Have a good day. I'll see you tomorrow. *(Guideline #3: See the big picture.)*

As in this example, it's wise to prompt the student to articulate his intentions. I've found that students are more likely to follow a direction they give themselves than one a teacher gives them.

Sometimes misbehaving students won't be so cooperative. What if you ask a student to step aside for a private conversation and he refuses? This is where a minor offense, like rowdy behavior in the hallway, becomes a major one: direct defiance of a teacher. In these situations, the best bet is to remain calm and not escalate the problem further by trying to "show the kid who's boss" or being rude in return. I follow the student until he enters his next class or goes to his locker or until I see a security guard or an administrator. If I get to his class, wonderful. Now he is with a teacher who knows him and can detain him. I get the student's name and then write a referral. If the situation calls for security to remove the student right then and there, I explain the situation to the student's classroom teacher and ask him or her to please call security. I stick around to speak with the security guard myself if I have a planning period at that time or if I do not trust the classroom teacher to convey the information.

Classroom Noise

Serenity comes not alone by removing the outward causes and occasions of fear, but by the discovery of inward reservoirs to draw upon.

—Rufus M. Jones

I used to think that my students had no call to ever talk in my class. Didn't they have plenty of time to talk in the halls, on the bus, at lunch, and at night on the phone? Now I realize that teenagers *never* have enough time to talk! They really are social creatures who need to connect with one another. My solution is to give them an opportunity to chat at the beginning and end of my class. In the beginning of class, they have about two minutes while I take roll, conduct a book check, and collect attendance paperwork. Then, at the end of the class period, after I have summarized what we did and have announced what we will be doing tomorrow, any extra time—usually no more than three minutes—is theirs. I build this system starting on the first day, and the students get comfortable with it. They do not fight what they are used to.

Of course, even when there is a time set aside for conversation, you will encounter talkers. One of the most familiar situations is the pair of students who talk incessantly. Address this by holding a private, three-person meeting. I recommend the following approach:

> *Teacher:* I am having difficulty teaching you two and the rest of the class because of your constant talking. I know it is difficult to sit near a close friend without talking. *(Guideline #2: Stay focused on the problem.)*

Pause, and give the students time to respond. Remember, these are talkers; if you give them room, they will open up. After they respond, or if the silence goes on too long, continue the conversation:

> *Teacher:* You two have shown me how mature you can be, and I trust that this maturity can be shown again. Do you think you can try to stop the talking, and we will meet back in a week and see how it's going? *(Guideline #3: See the big picture.)*

Or try this:

> *Teacher:* What kind of options can we come up with to resolve this issue? *(Guideline #3: See the big picture.)*

At this point, the goal is to get the talkers to commit to change. If they slip up during the following week, a simple, nonverbal intervention usually gets them back on the right track.

Another way to channel students' talkativeness and need to connect with one another is by incorporating cooperative learning into your lessons at points where it will enhance the learning process. Of course, this raises additional, noise-related issues.

Early in my career, a colleague shared many pieces of advice with me, and one of the most valuable was "do not talk over your students." It's especially important to remember this during cooperative learning exercises, where talking is not only allowed but essential. When I need to get the class's attention, I always say "Excuse me." Then I give everyone a few seconds to finish their conversations; after all, I *did* just interrupt their work. I wait until all eyes are on me, pencils are down, and mouths are not talking. Then I talk *to* them, not over them. Remember, though: Students who are interrupted too often are going to get agitated, just as anyone would, and their work will suffer. Respect them and they will usually reciprocate.

After modeling this attention-getting approach a few times, you'll find that students are able to come to order and calm themselves more quickly. Because they are calmer, they are more reasonable, and because they are more reasonable, they are able to think more logically and creatively. This is a stair-step approach to classroom management that all students respond to well. My student Shaynelle supported this in her closing letter: "It was wonderful to leave the day from an organized, settled class period."

It's true that some students respond well to disorganization, but I have never met one who could not work in an organized classroom. Noise is no longer a concern when students know when I will allow talking and what kind of talking will be accepted. They know they will get an opportunity to talk, and they understand that the teacher will not speak unless she will be heard. They learn to respect the teacher's words, just as the teacher shows her respect for theirs by listening to them and maintaining that same quiet in the classroom when they speak.

Off-Task Group Work

By prevailing over all obstacles and distractions, one may unfailingly arrive at his chosen goal or destination.
—Christopher Columbus

Any teacher who uses group work has experienced the challenge of keeping students on task. It is essential to establish firm guidelines for every cooperative learning assignment. At the beginning of the school year, my cooperative work groups are always teacher-selected, and I continue to choose who will work together until I am sure the class will respect my assignments and the working guidelines enough to do a good job with a friend or in groups of three or four.

Monitoring is key to keeping students focused. Although some kids will try to convince me that they can work on the assignment *and* talk about what they're going to do after school or where they're going out this weekend, I've learned not to budge. I've also learned that threats ("If you don't follow the rules, you won't be allowed to work in groups again!") aren't useful. It's better to simply communicate what I need: "In order for me to feel comfortable with this kind of assignment, I have to see and hear that everyone is working." *(Guideline #2: Stay focused on the problem.)* My students know they are free to talk about the assignment provided they do so at a conversational level. If they have questions or disagreements, instead of shouting out for my attention, they must raise their hands.

Proper directions are the other half of the equation. A good approach is to assign each student a specific task or role. One might be the "recorder," charged with taking notes, and the other might be the "word definer," or whatever else the assignment calls for. I distribute written guidelines detailing the tasks and responsibilities of each role and ensure there is enough work for each role player to do. One way to prevent one workgroup partner from taking advantage of the other is to insist that each student create and turn in an individual response sheet or some other sort of product.

Cooperative learning is not like baking a cake. You can't just take an assignment, add two to four kids, and reasonably expect an enriching learning experience to emerge every time. Group work requires constant oversight and continual tweaking. I walk around, listen, and watch. First, the students see me doing this and are less likely to begin off-task behaviors. Second, if they do begin off-task behaviors, I can stop them when they start.

If a group is simply not working after 15 minutes of me answering questions and asking for cooperation, I break up the group and direct them to complete parts of the assignment on their own. I do not make threats about doing this; I do it. The other students appreciate that I have silenced the distracting group *and* that I hold each group accountable to the same standards of behavior. The kids in the group I've dismantled understand that I am serious about them learning from this assignment, with or without a group.

Cooperative Work That's Less Than Cooperative

There is a loftier ambition than merely to stand high in the world.
It is to stoop down and lift mankind a little higher.
—Henry Van Dyke

Adolescent students are smart. They have been in a classroom setting almost all of their lives, and they know how the system works. Just because a cooperative learning lesson plan calls for them to approach and complete an assignment in a certain manner doesn't mean they will do exactly that.

This is why teachers must be very explicit about expectations for group work. I tell my students what I want them to do and what I hope they will get out of it. Then I distribute assignment sheets with a written version of the explanation I've just given. This way, if they choose to deviate from the directions, they have accepted the possibility of getting a lower grade. If I am unclear about the assignment, then they feel justified in getting mad at me when I respond negatively to a divergent approach they decided to take.

One approach my students frequently attempt is "divide and conquer." Given a set of questions to discuss and reach consensus on, they simply divide the items among themselves and take turns copying answers from each other. When I suspect this is going on, I pull up a desk and innocently ask, "OK, group, what number are you on?" This catches them off guard, but it can get them back on track. I stay with them until they have discussed at least one question without much input from me. I do make sure they understand how to discuss these questions, use available resources to back up their hunches, and decide on an answer.

Another classic approach to escaping work during cooperative learning exercises is to simply give all the work to the group's smartest or most diligent member and then copy off him or her at the end of the period. This student winds up resenting doing all the work and resenting the teacher who allowed this to happen. If there is only one kid doing the assignment, what are the other kids doing? Talking, sleeping, finishing math homework, and daydreaming. Joining the group and working with students for two or three problems helps ward off this problem too. Of course, when sitting with any particular group, you must not forget to keep an eye on the others. After a group exercise, consider asking students questions at random to ascertain their level of participation, and assign grades accordingly.

"Undersupplied" Students

True life is lived when tiny changes occur.

—Leo Tolstoy

When a student shows up in my class without school supplies, I have a difficult time being upset. For many of my kids, the family budget does not include funds for paper or notebooks or writing utensils, and being prepared for class often means relying on teachers, friends, and luck. They get used to hearing things like this: "What, *again?* How many times do I have to remind you to always bring ___?" "Chad, what are you thinking when you get up for school in the morning?" "No, you may not borrow a pencil. I'm sick of lending stuff to you."

This is a tough way to live 180 days of the year. It's no wonder so many students respond to this kind of disapproval with a variety of negative behaviors. Some stop asking for supplies and begin to sit and do nothing when they do not have what they need. Some get angry and rude if their requests aren't met immediately ("I *said,* I need a pen!"). Others simply lift their hand and move it in a writing motion or mumble, "Pen." These behaviors can be very annoying, but annoying or not, we must deal with them in a positive way.

Here's what I do. For the student who would rather look uncooperative than unprepared, I bring over what he needs without saying a word. The next time he needs something, maybe he will trust me enough to ask for it. For the angry student, I might look her in the eye and tell her that I will speak to her in just a moment. Once I can break from the class, I'll invite this student into the hallway for a private conference. It usually goes something like this:

Teacher: I become frustrated when you make demands on me. I would like for you to come to class prepared, but if you cannot, then you will have to wait patiently until I have a chance to help you. *(Guideline #2: Stay focused on the problem.)*

Student: I didn't mean to frustrate you, but I was getting behind in taking notes.

Teacher: Sounds as though you were becoming frustrated too. *(Guideline #3: See the big picture.)*

Student: Yeah. I guess I need to find a way to keep supplies with me so I can pass.

Teacher: How do you think you can do it? *(Guideline #2: Stay focused on the problem.)*

Student: If I remember to put my pencil in the pocket of my book bag, then I won't have trouble finding it and I won't lose it. But then my brother can steal it when I get home.

Teacher: Hmm.

Student: Maybe I could put it on the top shelf of my locker until the next day.

Teacher: I think this sounds like a good plan. Now, let's go back in, and I'll lend you a pen for today. *(Guideline #4: Don't sell out your values.)*

What I want is for this student to understand my concern and come up with a solution. I remind myself that my role is not to solve the student's problem but to offer a forum where she is comfortable enough to throw out ideas and form a plan that she is willing to stick to. It's doubtful that any solution I could come up with would work as well.

The student I mentioned who writes in the air with his hand or just says "Pen," can sometimes be dealt with through humor. I might make the same motion with my hand and say, "Yeah. You're right. This does help with wrist cramps." Or I might look at him and say, "*Cil*. Pen-*cil*. That's right—*pencil* is a two-syllable word."

The student will usually laugh and ask, "May I borrow a pencil?"

To that I will reply, "Oh, is *that* what you were trying to communicate? I'd say your last choice was most effective." *(Guideline #2: Stay focused on the problem.)* Then I lend him something to write with, and we get back to the lesson.

If a student is not good about returning what he has borrowed, I insist on collateral. It could be anything: a piece of candy, a math book, a ring. Typically, three good things come out of this practice:

1. The student learns a new vocabulary word (*collateral:* property pledged by a borrower to protect the interests of the lender).
2. The student learns to return borrowed items.
3. The student learns that things are earned, not simply given.

There will always be variations on how students respond to being unprepared, but if I remember to see each student as an individual, I can deal with their "undersupplied" status and isolate it from irresponsibility, laziness, or apathy. Prompted by my caring response, and wanting to respond to that care, these students change their behavior in a positive way.

Food and Drink in Class

Take time to deliberate, but when the time for action arrives, stop thinking and go in.

—Andrew Jackson

Teachers can stop students from bringing food or drink into the classroom simply by insisting that students throw these items away when they walk in the door. Sure, some students will be sly and hide their Burger King bags, orange juice, or soda in their backpacks, but if you cannot see it, they cannot eat it. With food that students can eat quickly—things like hard candy and miniature candy bars—just raise an eyebrow, have them throw away the wrapper, and make sure they have no more.

I set up the "throw it out" rule at the beginning of the school year, clarifying that I am not here to waste anyone's money by having them throw out food or beverages, but neither am I willing to fight these things for their attention. With consistent enforcement, the amount of food entering the classroom soon slows to a trickle. And because I do not want my students to eat or drink in class, I abide by the same rules. I might have a soda or throw a mint in my mouth between classes, but I am sure to finish it by the time the next class is in my room.

It's irresponsible to talk about the topic of eating in class without acknowledging that more students than we might imagine are attempting to learn on an empty stomach. Poor nutrition can cause poor behavior. Imagine attending seven classes, mingling with friends and enemies, and trying to learn when your stomach is growling. Even the most level-headed adult would struggle to stay alert and polite under these circumstances. An adolescent from a home where dinner the night before was a handful of Ruffles and breakfast was nonexistent is not going to cope well in the classroom. We need to keep this in mind with kids who seem sullen, sleepy, angry, or defensive. They could need some food to get them on track.

I once taught a student who had grown up far too fast. She was 14 years old and already a mother. She had a 19-year-old boyfriend and a permissive parent. She was also rude and argumentative. I asked her to stay after class one day, after my usual discipline steps to curb her poor behavior had failed.

Following a hunch, I asked her, "Did you eat breakfast this morning?"

"No," she admitted. "My mama ain't got any food in the house."

"Would you like some peanut butter crackers to hold you over until lunchtime?"

She nodded, and I pulled out a package of crackers.

"Thank you, Ms. Ridnouer," she said in a surprised voice.

I told her it was no problem and wrote her a pass to her next class.

This student began to keep her comments to herself and to be less demanding on my time. By focusing on the problem *(Guideline #2)* and staying true to my values *(Guideline #4)*, I was able to reach this girl, who was allowing her hunger to control her behavior. Now, I always keep a box of peanut butter cracker packages in my desk to help that student who needs a little energy to survive the day.

Speech That's Hard to Understand

It don't mean a thing if it ain't got that swing.
—Duke Ellington and Irving Mills

My students speak with a strong regional dialect that strays from "correct" grammar and syntax. This can slow our classroom communication and frustrate everybody involved. Other teachers might encounter similar difficulties when they have students who are just acquiring the English language or even prone to using lots of slang that's impenetrable to adult ears. Because my students communicate effectively with their family and friends, they have a difficult time understanding why I do not always understand them. I try to meet them halfway, so their feelings do not get hurt, and they learn to change their speaking habits at least when they speak to me.

This can be a touchy endeavor. Many of my students hear non-standard English all day from their family, friends, other teachers, co-workers, bosses, and bus drivers. If the student can understand and be understood by these people, they want to know what's the point of changing how they talk?

It's a good question. My answer is, "When you're sitting in that leather chair talking to the president of a large corporation about why he should hire you, don't allow your poor English to scream, 'Don't hire me!' No matter what you actually say, if your English is poor, *that's* what the president will hear." I go on to explain that I realize they speak one way at home and another way in my class, and that's OK. *But* they need to learn to turn informal and formal speech on and off, just as they modify their actions and behavior, depending on the situation.

I do not judge my students when they don't enunciate or when they make a grammatical or syntactical mistake in their speech. I simply ask them to repeat themselves, slowly. If the student is in a receptive mood, I might offer a correction, but otherwise I focus on responding to whatever he was trying to communicate. I also write down the most common mistakes I hear my students make and maintain an ongoing list. Occasionally, on days that my lesson runs short, I write these mistakes on the board and ask the students to work cooperatively to transform them into "proper English." My kids love this exercise.

Poor Attendance

In today already walks tomorrow.
—Samuel Taylor Coleridge

At my school, we take the official attendance in third period. Each day I typically turn in at least three absence cards—usually the *same* three cards for the same three students. I send notices of excessive absences and I call home. The parents say, "She's decided to drop out and there's no way I can change her mind," or, "I'll try to get him to school, but he's pig-headed." Sometimes the parents' phone is disconnected or I have the wrong number. In most cases, my efforts are in vain. These students are not coming to school.

This is not to say that teachers should *stop* trying to reach students who are chronically absent. Of course we should all follow the steps our school has set up to address excessive absenteeism. However, it just doesn't make sense for us to beat ourselves up about those students who don't come to class. We should reserve our energy for those who do; they are the ones we can teach, reach, and shape into future leaders.

Outside Interruptions

Did you ever observe to whom the accidents happen? Chance favors only the prepared mind.

—Louis Pasteur

How often when you are teaching will you hear a knock on the door 'and open it to find a student wanting to speak to someone in your class? When it happens to me, my first impulse is to lecture that student on how valuable my class time is and how she is wasting it. Of course, this would only waste more time and give the student a person to hate: me. So instead, I *show* the student that I will not waste class time. In an even tone of voice, I announce that I do not allow class interruptions. I say it quickly and then I shut the door. Do this consistently and outside interruptions will become less of a problem.

Poor Concentration

Learning is a form of accepting.

—Stella Terrill Mann

My regular-level students differ from my advanced students in a variety of ways, but one aspect that always stands out is their struggle to focus on one task throughout an entire class period. With my advanced class, I can introduce a lesson, give directions, clarify expectations, and let the students work until I interrupt them. Not so with my regular students. They are at their best when I plan two, three, or four different activities for one class period. This is an arduous task, and I admit that some days we simply have to focus on one activity to finish a unit or complete a lesson.

As the year progresses, I lengthen each activity's duration, thereby reducing the number of activities possible in the class period. I also make sure to give time limits, which include starting and ending times. If I plan to have students finish a class assignment for homework, but they have 15 minutes to start on it, I don't tell them it is homework until I tell them to stop for the day. I am tricking them in a sense, but when I do tell them it is homework, they are relieved because they have already gotten a head start on the assignment.

Strange Clothing Habits

The true mystery of the world is the visible, not the invisible.
—Oscar Wilde

It was a puzzling phenomenon: students who opted to sweat through class instead of taking off the heavy winter coats they were wearing. As I came to understand my students better, I began to understand the situation. The starter jackets they wore to announce their professional sports allegiances were too bulky to fit in their lockers. There was nowhere to leave these jackets unless they entrusted them to a teacher, which would require asking permission and risking that the jacket would be stolen anyway. Once these students weighed those odds against listening to their parents gripe about a stolen jacket and having to freeze for the next few months, wearing their coats all day became the easiest, safest choice.

Why is this phenomenon a challenge for teachers? Well, it's not, if students accept that wearing a coat all day long has consequences—like burning up in a heated winter classroom. But this doesn't occur to some students, especially self-focused, teenage ones. They expect each classroom's temperature to be just right for them, and if it's not, you've got trouble.

John was a junior who sat by one of the classroom cooling units and had figured out how to use his pencil to adjust the unit's temperature setting. Yes, John wore his starter jacket all day long. To make matters worse, he came to my class after PE and always had a glow of sweat about him. John would blast the cold air in the middle of November. Meanwhile, students who were dressed appropriately were sitting there shivering. After tolerating this for some time, they finally got sick of it and lodged a complaint.

I went to John and handed him the temperature-adjustment knob, which I kept in my desk. "I need you to turn that air off," I said. "Look at Melanie; she's turning into a popsicle." *(Guideline #2: Stay focused on the problem.)*

Instead of being reasonable, John got angry. "I don't care if she's freezing!" he yelled. "I'm burning up!"

Time for a private conversation in the hallway. "Pick up your things and follow me," I replied. *(Guideline #4: Don't sell out your values.)* Once we were outside the classroom, I explained what I needed: "John, you'll need to take your coat off if you're hot."

He didn't say a word.

"John, it's not fair that everyone around you has to freeze because you choose to wear your jacket all period." *(Guideline #2: Stay focused on the problem.)*

It was then that I noticed the dingy, yellowed undershirt that he was wearing under his open jacket. It was the same undershirt he had worn yesterday and the day before that. This was when I found out the second reason why students sometimes wear temperature-inappropriate coats. John was embarrassed about his clothes, but he was proud of his starter jacket.

I was in a bind. I couldn't force the other kids to suffer, but I couldn't force John to take off that jacket either. So I gave him the choice.

"John, how can we solve this problem?" I asked. *(Guideline #2: Stay focused on the problem.)*

"I dunno."

"How about you choose from these options? Option 1 is I'll let you remain sitting in your assigned seat, and you'll remove your jacket and leave the air off. Option 2 is I'll change your seat so you can't choose to make other people miserable. These aren't very good choices, but they're all I can think of. Can you think of anything else?" *(Guideline #3: See the big picture.)*

"No," John said. "Just move me."

That's what I did, and he seemed to wean himself off that jacket slowly.

I use this same technique with girls who wear spaghetti-strap tank tops in May and wonder why they are freezing. The reasonable ones keep a light sweater in their backpacks, while the less reasonable ones try to complain. They stop when I just look at them and say nothing.

If you face these kinds of clothing issues, I recommend adding a new topic to your beginning-of-the-year discussion with students. Talk about clothing choices and how the group is more important than the individual in the matter of room temperature. Remind students of this in the spring, when they show up in skimpy clothes, so there is nothing to discuss when they are freezing. Do not let their poor choices make everyone else uncomfortable.

Disrespectful Language

Have I really pushed the envelope as much as I want to? Not yet.
Maybe that's why I'm still hungry.

—Steven Spielberg

Every day I walk down the hall and hear, "Shut up, you stupid ho!" The girl who says it might be talking to her best friend, and they both have smiles on their faces. This is how they talk to each other. If I catch their attention, I raise my eyebrows to show my surprise, but I generally do not address it any further than that.

When students speak to each other in this manner in my classroom, however, I do address it. During the first week of school, I tell students how I will react if I hear negative remarks in my classroom. I tell them that I don't care what their friends, moms, dads, or other teachers allow them to say. I go on to explain that I will be respectful of everyone in the class, and I expect the same from them. I tell them I don't want to hear cursing, "Shut up!" "That's stupid!" or any other negative, dismissive, or disrespectful talk.

For some of my kids, these are very high expectations, but I insist upon them nonetheless. Again, the key is to set the expectation and be consistent about enforcing it. When one of my students slips, I respond with my basic discipline steps: a nonverbal warning, a verbal warning, a private conversation in the hallway, a parent phone call, and a referral to the office. At each point, the student involved may choose whether or not to continue the behavior, and I'm careful to show that each disrespectful choice brings consequences.

I have deviated from this approach occasionally, but only when I know a student well enough to understand that he responds better to humor or to another tactic than he does to nonverbal warnings. Lamar, for instance, had a very flavorful vocabulary full of descriptive words for people's mothers and personalities. When I heard Lamar tell one kid that he was a !@#$%& loser, I walked over to him and told him, loudly enough for both Lamar and the "loser" kid to hear, to please keep his adjectives to himself. He liked that, and he turned his attention away from the boy. A win–win.

When a student speaks disrespectfully to a teacher, he is usually doing it to redirect the real source of his frustration. Perhaps he is upset because his parents are fighting each night, his math class is a jumble of numbers, or he just failed his driving test. The keys are to respond to the student, not to his behavior *(Guideline #2: Stay focused on the problem),* and to help the student verbalize the real trouble. A talk in the hallway might go like this:

Teacher: Mike, are you doing OK?
Mike: Great, just great.

Teacher: Mike, look at me, please, not at the floor. Can I help you with anything? *(Guideline #1: Don't let students fast-talk you.)*

Mike: I am fine. My parents aren't fine, but I'm fine.

Teacher: What's going on with your parents?

Mike: Oh, they're fighting, and I'm sick of it. I hope one of them just moves out so my sister and me can get some peace.

Teacher: Have you told your parents how you feel?

Mike: C'mon! I can't do that.

Teacher: All I know is that a respectful boy in my class named Mike was disrespectful today. *(Guideline #2: Stay focused on the problem.)* I know that's not how you want to be. I'm trying to help you. Please talk to your parents.

Mike: Well, I'll think about it. Oh, and I'm sorry for being disrespectful.

Incomplete Work and Poor Motivation

When you work you are a flute through whose heart the whispering of the hours turns to music.

—Kahlil Gibran

For many of my students, school is the only structured time in their day. They don't have a schedule to follow when they arrive home and are free to roam with their friends until all hours of the night. Half the time I feel honored when some of them *do* turn in homework and writing assignments despite having little pressure from home to do so and despite being tired and hungry.

I focus on influencing that which I can influence. One of the most important ways I can encourage students to focus on and complete their work is to provide interesting lessons and assignments that will not only help them meet the required standards but also show them that school is useful—a way for them to improve their lives. I want them to feel that they need to keep showing up and keep working hard.

I stress to my students that they are the ones who choose to be successful or not. Those who want to pass, I nag about due dates and late assignments. Those who have a difficult time choosing whether or not to even come to school, I nag less. I want to provide them with *knowledge,* which is a tool I know will help them survive. Not just knowledge about similes and metaphors, but also knowledge about themselves. And so, I bring in science, history, and math references for the literature we read. By commingling the subjects, I try to mimic the complexity of life and open my students' eyes to how all these "subjects" commingle in the real world outside of school. For example, when I teach *A Farewell to Arms,* I want them to see the relationship among war, the survival of the fittest, and geometry. Then, maybe, they might pick up on the parallel relationship among their mother's inability to secure a loving boyfriend and their own tendency to latch onto new people. The fact of the matter is I am trying to give them the gift of reflection, the gift of being able to see their lives within the context of something outside of their own experience. Once they can see themselves beyond their immediate surroundings, they can begin adapting their surroundings to suit their dreams.

I wish this were as easy as handing someone a mirror, but it's much more involved. That's why I am not afraid to bring in examples from my own life. I share with my students that when I was in 5th grade, I figured out what year I would graduate from college, and that was the year I *did* graduate from college. After that, we figure out when *they* will graduate from college. Maybe some of them will do what I did and use that date as motivation.

The students respond well to these discussions, as evidenced in a closing letter by a once-hostile girl named Felicia: "This year I really liked English. It has not always been my favorite subject, but the assignments that you gave made English interesting. A lot of times, English can be very boring, but I like how you interacted with us, such as having class discussions." Another student, Tamika, said this: "What I loved about English is when we as a class talked about anything and I am able to understand it better." She ended her letter with a postscript that touches my heart: "Not only were you our teacher, you were also our friend."

Felicia, Tamika, their classmates, and I were all able to see each other as people and not get lost in the usual teacher-student difficulties. This is the pinnacle. When students can learn from a teacher, feel that the teacher cares about them, and see that teacher as a person, they are ready for the world. This understanding of relationships will help them succeed in love, work, and social relationships.

Questions for Reflection

1. How do you expect your students to behave when they are in the hallways or otherwise not under a specific person's supervision? How do you enforce this expectation?

2. How do you manage noise in your classroom?

3. What do you do when students working in a group get off task?

4. What do you do when your students come to class without school supplies?

5. What do you do when students bring food or drink into your classroom?

6. What do you do when a student comes to class tired or hungry?

7. What do you do when a student's speech is difficult to understand?

8. What is your response to a student's poor attendance?

9. How do you help your students concentrate?

10. How does recognizing and addressing a student's problem affect his ability to learn from you? How does it affect your ability to teach him in the future?

5

Giving Kids What They Need

There is only one real deprivation . . . and that is not to be able to give one's gifts to those one loves most.

—May Sarton

Each of the students sitting in your classroom requires something from you. Maybe some need a boost in their self-esteem, their confidence, or their reading ability. Probably others just want you to leave alone and teach the subject matter. Nurturing these students is a matter of figuring out each student's needs and then giving the kind of attention that will help the most.

Confidence

Whether you believe you can do a thing or not, you are right.
—Henry Ford

Rick was a student who did not display much confidence in himself at the beginning of the year. By the end of the year, all that had changed, and he wrote, "At times I still maybe get something incorrect but that's just a matter of practice." I do not remember stressing practice to Rick, except perhaps when I insisted he write multiple drafts of each essay and research paper. But I do remember the day that I first saw the light of confidence shining in his eyes.

I had just finished passing out papers, and Rick raised his hand and asked, "Ms. Ridnouer, where's my paper?"

"It's hanging on the wall, Rick," I told him. "I thought you saw it up there."

"What? It is? Can I go look at it?"

"Of course. Go quickly."

It was a great moment: a 17-year-old giggling like a little kid because he'd earned an *A–* on a paper, and I'd posted his work for everyone to see. In a matter of a minute Rick transformed his perception of himself from a loser to a winner. He gave himself the gift of confidence.

Brian was another who lacked confidence. While writing, time and time again he would allow himself to get so mired in proving a point that he would find himself stuck, pencil in hand. I could almost see his mind trying to come up with the next thought.

"Skip it and move on to the next paragraph," I told him. "When you come back to it, you'll be able to process that thought."

I don't know if he believed me, but he did it anyway. This one little strategy changed everything about Brian's approach to his writing. From that day on, he was able to write fantastic, assured papers. In his closing letter, Brian wrote that the most important thing he had learned in my class was that "it was OK to make mistakes as long as you learn from them."

Rick and Brian both gained confidence when they were prompted to rethink a pattern of thought established long before they entered my classroom. Like too many students, they believed that success in school should come easily to them, and if it didn't, it never would. The way past this is to teach students to analyze their own work and to expect to find imperfections. When they can quiet the distracting "I'm no good at this" voice in their brains, they realize that they really can do anything they set out to do, provided they allow themselves time to practice and learn and practice again.

In his book *Schools Without Failure,* William Glasser makes an important distinction between people who fail and people who succeed—one that I see proven every day in my students, coworkers, and people in general. Glasser writes, "People who fail fall back upon emotion to direct their behavior; people who succeed rely upon reason and logic" (p. 20).* It takes a calm mind to access reason and logic, and it is difficult to be calm in a chaotic or confrontational classroom. We promote our students' success when we provide a structure that allows them to be calm and feel safe, so that reason and logic may dominate their analysis of their work and themselves.

My principal, like many, has an appreciation for "controlled chaos." Some teachers misunderstand this to mean that yelling and screaming are acceptable behaviors. I take it to mean that if an administrator walks into my class, he might see us having a discussion that moves rapidly, and he might see that students don't always raise their hands before they speak. But I do insist that my students follow some basic rules: no interruptions, no rude remarks, and no off-task behavior. When students know what is expected of them and what is out of bounds, they'll work well, even in a fast-paced setting. Without the ground rules, tempers flare and feelings get hurt; with them, students feel secure enough to open themselves up to reflection.

A Connection with the Curriculum

> *Our aspirations are our possibilities.*
>
> —Samuel Johnson

I don't have to tell you that it can be difficult to get modern teenagers excited about Nathanial Hawthorne and Ralph Waldo Emerson. My

---

*Glasser, W. (1975). *Schools without failure.* New York: Harper Paperbacks.

students, many of whom come from rough home environments, look at the authors on our English syllabus and ask, "What do these people have to do with our lives?"

It's a good question. We work together to answer it by pulling out the themes of love, frustration, and peer pressure, and my students begin to feel a little bit connected to these long-dead writers. I want more.

We move on to Thoreau and study excerpts of *Walden*. At first, they don't get it. Again they ask, "What does he have to do with us?" In response, I ask them to turn to the famous lines in which Thoreau explains the true purpose behind his withdrawal from society: "I went to the woods because I wished to live deliberately, to front only the essential facts of life, and see if I could not learn what it had to teach, and not, when I came to die, discover that I had not lived."

I ask all my students to memorize these lines and inform them that they will have to reproduce the lines perfectly for a quiz grade. When we first read them together, a look of "So?" runs across almost every face. To begin, I launch a discussion of the word *deliberately*. I ask, "What does a judge do during deliberation?" and "How can life be lived deliberately?" We answer these questions and discuss the various responses the students have. Then, we attempt to define the "essential facts" of their lives. They start off a little flippant: The essential facts of their lives are that they are their parents' official babysitters, that school is a jail, that they hate their siblings, that they wish they had more money. Then we move into the serious: "I am a great dancer." "Nobody blocks like I do on the football field." "I just want my mom to be well." "I hope my sister is safe. She ran away, and we don't know where she is." They begin to understand that purposeful living for Thoreau might not be purposeful living for them, but the motivation behind it is the same.

The week we are studying for the Thoreau quiz, I greet students at the door with the question, "Now why did you go to the woods?" Some get it immediately and reply, "Because I wished to live deliberately!" From others, I get a strange look and a confused denial: "What? I didn't go to the woods!" Then they see my smile and the smiles on the surrounding students' faces, and recognition kicks in: "Oh yeah, something about *deliberately.*" Once in a while, another kid will chime in, "It's because you wanted to live deliberately, to front only the essential facts of life. *C'mon,* man!" I never say a word when this happens; I just smile, smile, smile.

The ultimate purpose of this kind of pre-class interaction is to show the kids that I think about the material beyond our 48-minute slot, and it is OK for them to do so too. Incidentally, most of my students earn an *A* on the Thoreau quiz. They like the idea of transcending.

My husband's uncle, Jake McCaffery, was a math teacher for 40 years. Talking to him about teaching always renews my love for the profession I've chosen. He compares life in front of a class of high school students to the life of an actor on stage. We have to be interesting enough to gain their attention; we have to be passionate enough to strike love for the subject in their hearts; and we have to be human enough for them to connect with what we are saying. There's no denying that this takes a lot of energy and a lot of planning, but when my head is buzzing from my second period students talking about apostrophes and pronouns with the same energy that they have when they talk about fingernails and clothing, I know I have had an outstanding performance. The buzz in my ears is my standing ovation.

A Model of Self-Control

We must be willing to get rid of the life we've planned, so as to have the life that is waiting for us.
—Joseph Campbell

I once had a girl named Tanya in my homeroom. She was striking, with big eyes, dark skin, a nose ring, and a jaw as big as Carly Simon's. She also seemed to feel that a breakfast stop at Burger King was more important than showing up in homeroom. When Tanya *was* present, she complained. The room was too hot or too cold; the announcements were too long; homeroom was useless.

My usual homeroom routine includes discussing upcoming school events or any concerns my students might have. Tanya always chimed in with her thoughts, interrupting other students and me without compunction. I would follow my usual steps: a nonverbal warning, a verbal warning, and a private discussion in the hallway. (Because I only saw her once a week, calling home wouldn't have been effective, and her behavior was rarely "bad" enough to warrant a referral to the office.) I remember one of our discussions very vividly. Tanya's excuse for her behavior was that she had no control over herself.

"If you can't control yourself, who does control you?" I asked her.

"Nobody," she said.

"Wow. So who is accountable for your actions?"

"Ms. Ridnouer, you don't make no sense," she informed me. The bell rang and our conversation was over.

I attempt to teach the students in my classes to follow a course different from Tanya's, and I do this by modeling self-awareness. If I am having a bad day, I tell them. If I am getting lost during an explanation, I note this out loud, collect my thoughts, and start over. I prompt students to follow my lead and be conscious of their own thought processes, behavior, attitude, and academic achievement. When a group of students is misbehaving or straying from the assignment, I ask, "What is wrong with this picture?" If a student is just staring into space, I might walk over, crouch down, and say, "Are you doing OK?" To the student moving to a beat that only he hears, I might walk over and say, "Give me the energy in the discussion."

Self-monitoring will only occur in an environment where a student is comfortable and trusts the person leading the group. Trust is a difficult issue for many teenagers, and for those like my students, who have been on the losing end of so many broken promises, it's even tougher. Initially, they don't believe me when I say, "You will succeed in this class," and "I am here when you need me." Why should they? And so they test me, and I must make sure that I'm ready for the assessment. If I talk to a student about excessive absenteeism, can he accuse *me* of excessive absenteeism? Am *I* unprepared? Am

I tardy? Am I disorganized? Am I unreasonable? Am I rude? Am I a rule breaker? Am I disrespectful to my boss or to the students I teach? Am I sick of challenges? The answer to all these questions must be no.

I know that no teacher is perfect, but we all bear the responsibility of being the best that we can be. We should strive to improve our organization skills, to design more interesting lesson plans, to learn more, to be more considerate, and to be more trustworthy. It all comes down to being a good person. I am not talking about following a certain religion or being a certain kind of citizen. What I mean is that we must strive to grow as people through our interactions with our students. Settling on a set reaction for certain offenses or to "types" of kids or opting for inflexible lesson plans prevents this growth. That's when teaching becomes just a job, a chore, a bore.

A Sympathetic Ear

You can have anything you want if you want it desperately enough.
You must want it with an exuberance that erupts through the skin
and joins the energy that created the world.

—Sheila Graham

Often students will approach teachers under the guise of wanting help with schoolwork when what they really want is someone to talk to. I believe it's a teacher's responsibility to listen when a student has a problem. When my students share their struggles with me, I do not criticize or try to "make it all better," but I do ask questions and show empathy.

One of my 11th graders, Tamika, was pregnant and missed a lot of days during her first trimester. When she did come to school, I encouraged her to come see me at lunch to talk about her make-up work. Initially she backed away and said she would get the assignments from the assignment board, but I did not stop encouraging her to come at lunchtime. She needed more guidance than the homework board could provide.

Finally, Tamika took me up on my offer and showed up with her lunch in one hand and a notebook in the other. We began talking about the assignments, but it wasn't long before she started talking about her pregnancy. She was embarrassed and confused. Instead of telling her how to feel, I asked her questions. She responded with full answers, and I simply listened and ate my lunch, nodding my head every once in a while.

These lunchtime meetings continued for a while, and we were able to discuss issues beyond Tamika's pregnancy. Evidently, she had struggled with reading for years. This, she said, was why she felt that my class, English, was her worst subject. I explained to her that I wanted to help her change her mind about that. During lunch, Tamika and I started reading together. The words she had a tough time with, we broke into syllables, which she sounded out. It became clear that she had all the requisite decoding skills but lacked the confidence to implement them. As Tamika broke down the "reading wall," she was also able to break down the writing wall and the public speaking wall. Of course, she had the power to do this all along, just as Dorothy in *The Wizard of Oz* always had the power to go back to Kansas. Both girls just needed a little guidance.

When a student comes to you with a problem, it can be tempting to simply tell the student how *you* would handle the situation. I've learned that this is not a very effective strategy. Students can easily find ways to differentiate themselves from their teachers and what their teachers would do, and it's likely they'll have many reasons why they cannot implement *our* solutions. If they come up with solutions on their own, they're more likely to try them out.

I have also learned that if I make myself available to students, the students will come. Everyone recognizes a sympathetic ear and most troubled people gravitate toward it. In being the sympathetic ear, I am showing how much I care about my students. This has a powerful effect on my classroom dynamic because I gain students who trust my questioning and will respond honestly and thoughtfully. They won't give answers that they think I want to hear. They will tell me what they really think because, although I might have an answer in mind, I am flexible enough to accept other answers. As other students see this communication take place, they too feel safe enough to begin interacting with more honesty and reflection.

A Sense of Possibility

There are only hints and guesses,
Hints followed by guesses, and the rest
Is prayer, observance, discipline, thought and action.
—T. S. Eliot

So many high school students think of themselves in black and white terms: "I'm good," "I'm bad," "I'm smart," "I'm stupid." With each choice they make and action they take, they validate or invalidate the labels they decide to give themselves. As adults, we recognize that nobody is all one thing, whether it be good or bad, smart or stupid. We know when we have been "good" and we know when we have been "stupid." Students are just building the life experience that they need to figure this out.

To teach this valuable lesson to my students, I share stories about people who were once perceived negatively and are now perceived positively. I tell them about Maya Angelou, who was a prostitute and had a baby when she was an unmarried 18-year-old. Now she is a prize-winning author and a respected speaker, to name just a few of her accolades. I talk about my sister Polly, who was rather wild in her high school years: She did drugs, dated a drug dealer, was kicked out of our house, and barely graduated. Now she is a clinical psychologist, is married to a wonderful man, and has three lovely children. I talk about how she went to community college in her 20s and found that the biggest hurdle she faced was not the schoolwork but the confidence to *do* the schoolwork. She had to believe in herself by forgetting "the old Polly" and defining "the new Polly." She is now more confident than ever.

I use my sister as a running example in my classes for two reasons: My students love a personal story, and Polly's illustrates that individuals can change who they are and become who they want to be. I am continually surprised that many of my students claim to have no dreams, no goals. They seem so apathetic about their lives. So I give them journal prompts designed to strike a nerve and stir them out of their apathy ("What would you do if someone punched your mama?" "What if I stole your coat?" "What if I told you that you were stupid?"), and I encourage them to respond as honestly and as rudely as they want to. After a short discussion about these personal topics, they seem more willing to state and defend opinions about the lesson-related topic. They are beginning to form an identity that is more than a reaction to their environment. When they can see who they are, they can begin to see who they want to become.

I also say things like this: "You are going to make a fine mathematician with thinking like that," or "They better watch out for you in the courtroom. As a lawyer, you'll light the place on fire." Sometimes my students smile, pleased by the compliment, and sometimes they say, "I ain't gonna be no lawyer," but at least they react. The reaction is what I am looking for. And if they react against my prediction, they are more likely to keep thinking about what they *are* going to be.

I listen for hints about what my students might want to study in college and bring them articles from the newspaper about someone in that field. I bring in entry forms for essay contests and oratorical contests, college preparatory program applications, and summer internship applications. I target those students who seem least likely to know about these opportunities and most likely to benefit from them. It's pretty exciting to watch my influence positively change the pattern of a student's thinking.

Here's one example. I taught a junior named Benita who was very talented at styling hair. She won contests and spoke very highly of her cosmetology class. This young lady was also gifted in the academic arena, but she had to work at it, whereas her success in front of that beautician's mirror came easily. When I first met Benita, she had one goal: to become a beautician. The curious thing was, she always said this with fake enthusiasm, as if she was trying to convince herself that this was her only career option.

I suspected this career would not give Benita the level of intellectual challenge that she would need to have a happy life. I started complimenting her on her writing skills and her strong presentation skills. I mentioned that these are skills that a lawyer and a banker need to be successful. Slowly but surely, Benita expanded her dream. Then one day I overheard her say that she was going to be a beautician *while* she went to college. Music to my ears!

Benita relaxed into her studies and disciplined herself to get her hours for her cosmetology license, complete her homework, care for her younger sisters, and still work 30 hours a week at her job. Sometimes she fell behind in her schoolwork, but she always got back on track. She seemed to enjoy the challenge of juggling it all. All Benita needed was someone to help point out her strengths and to open her eyes to her endless possibilities.

Order

The one fact that I would cry from every housetop is this: The Good Life is waiting for us—here and now.

—B. F. Skinner

So many of my students are engaged in a struggle to keep the chaos in their home lives at bay. A chaotic home delays the development of logical thinking. This is a concept that took me a while to accept; then again, I was raised in a home where life had a definite pattern. We ate dinner together every night. We went to church every Sunday. We each had chores to do. My parents talked to my siblings and me thoughtfully and logically. We could predict our parents' reaction to indiscretions and achievements.

When I went to school, I expected school life to be as predictable as my home life. It was, and I was comfortable there. I could understand and follow the steps my teacher laid out in lessons and then reproduce those steps when it was my turn to practice each new skill. The instruction I received followed the same type of logical pattern I saw elsewhere in my life.

What about the child raised in a home that has no established pattern except inconsistency? She is slapped across the face for watching television all day when the laundry needs to be washed. She is yelled at for talking back to the teacher, but she is ignored when she earns straight *A*s on her report card. This child is given no direction; she is left to guess at the pattern in the chaos of her home.

Some students from chaotic homes love the structure they find at school. It's as though they can finally relax because they finally know what is coming from one day to the next. Other students find the structure confining and balk at the regimented class periods, the inflexible grading scale (no, 37 percent cannot be a passing grade), and the consistent responses to their behavior. We must teach both the structure-lovers and the structure-haters how to learn in this environment.

One of the key strategies is to turn each challenge into a series of steps. Starting at the beginning of the year, I model a system of learning that will help my students analyze their lessons. For example, when I teach how to fix a run-on sentence, I put the steps for analysis on the board and ask students to follow these steps to analyze a set of sentences. I read through the steps again, and the students write them down in their notes. Then they analyze a new set of sentences. Next, we review the work together, with me asking for volunteers to walk us through the steps. Afterward, the students tackle a third group of sentences *without* their notes, unless they are stuck. Finally, they take a quiz that asks them not only to use the steps to analyze some sentences but also to write down the steps in their own words at the beginning of the test.

This lesson serves two purposes and teaches organizational skills along with the grammatical one. It also gives us a model to follow. In subsequent lessons, I will say, "Let's break this into steps." I ask the students to verbalize the steps for me, and I record them on the board. If they cannot explain a step in simple terms, we analyze an example and return to the steps. This is a difficult task for many learners. It is easy to be able to do something, but explaining how to do it is something else entirely. I believe that if my students are truly to learn to do something, they must learn the steps that comprise it. This may seem obvious and not something that a teacher must teach, but it does support the philosophy that we must care about and provide a framework for our students. By teaching my kids the skills of order and analysis, I am teaching them something many of them will not get unless they get it from me. Because I am teaching it within the framework of English class, I am not condemning their home or shaming them or their parents. Once they become used to these skills, their thinking is clearer. Ultimately, this increases their ability to make sound decisions both inside and out of school.

Respect

Allow children to be happy in their own way, for what better way will they ever find?
— Samuel Johnson

Students and teachers are not so different. Like us, some of them are naturally passive and some of them are naturally aggressive. When I am faced with handling a discipline issue, I try to tease out what kind of personality I am dealing with. I can't expect every person to respond to all situations, challenges, prompts, and guidance the same way I would. My "normal" might not be their "normal." Recognizing these personality quirks shows respect for the student as an individual.

I should've kept this in mind when I was teaching Sharon and Dana. Sharon tended to say whatever was on her mind, while Dana barely spoke, even when spoken to. Sharon's garrulous tendencies began disrupting the class, so I asked her to stay after one day. It was true that Dana was the one Sharon was talking to, but it was also obvious that Sharon instigated and dominated all conversations between the two. Because of this, I did not ask Dana to stay behind.

Sharon got mad. "Why didn't Dana have to stay after class?" she demanded loudly. "Why are you picking on me?"

I was dumbfounded. Usually when I speak with a student one-on-one, she is quiet, calm, and reasonable. Sharon was anything but.

I attempted to explain my reasoning, but Sharon would not be quiet long enough to listen. Because of this, I told her that beginning the next day, she would have a new seating assignment. This *really* made her mad, because in this particular class, I only had 10 students and assigned seats had not been necessary.

"I will not sit in an assigned seat," Sharon stated.

This is when I referred her to an administrator. I will only reason with someone so long before it is obvious that she only wants what she perceives as her "rights" and will not deviate from that line of thinking.

The next day, Sharon came in with a note from her administrator asking that I give her one more chance in her old seat next to Dana. Without backup from the administration, I had to give in. Once again she talked to Dana. Once again I asked her to stay after class, but she left right after the bell rang. I referred her to the office again, and she was suspended for one week.

When Sharon returned after the suspension, she headed right for her old seat until I intervened and directed her to a new one. Now I was the enemy. Interestingly, Dana's performance improved greatly in Sharon's absence, and she visibly relaxed over the course of a week's time. I suspect if I would've simply moved Dana and left Sharon alone, then the whole problem would have been resolved in the beginning, with no enemies made, no referrals to the office, and both girls learning in the end.

Acceptance

The notes I handle no better than many pianists. But the pauses between the notes—ah, that is where the art resides.
—Artur Schnabel

"I would have *never* talked to a teacher that way." This is something I hear teachers say to each other all the time. I've said it too. But in conversation with adults who are not teachers, I have found that many of them *did* talk to teachers "that way." They confess to having been all those things that we teachers dread: surly, sarcastic, egotistical. Perhaps those of us who chose to become teachers had an innate respect for the teaching profession that other people just do not have.

Whatever the reason is, we cannot keep wishing for a certain type of student. We have to train our eyes and ears to be more sensitive to the positive qualities in the students we do have. I used to cringe when I heard the kids laughing, joking, and yelling down the hall first thing in the morning. "They're so loud!" I would think to myself. I have since learned to pause and appreciate their energy. I see it as fuel that will ignite learning in my classroom. I know they have it; I just have to find a way to tap into it.

A problem rarely lasts when people deal with it directly, one-on-one. Look at social class barriers, for example. The student with the Coach bag might never set out to befriend the girl with unkempt hair and dirty shoes. But, as I've seen, when they are paired up for a project and required to interview one another about their lives, they see that they're not so different at all. As soon as they learn they both have a big brother, love dogs, or secretly wish to drag race, they become friends. As I sit down and discuss a problem directly, I get closer and closer to solving the problem. Getting angry every time I see a kid whose behavior or habits bother me means separating myself further from my students. It means they learn less about the subject I teach and more about intolerance.

So what's the answer? Wait for some magic to transpire so that I am no longer bothered by student sarcasm, surliness, egotism, or other particular behaviors? That magic isn't coming. The only option is to *decide* I will no longer allow those things to bother me. Doing otherwise means leaving myself open to reflexive anger any time those behaviors pop up. I'm a teacher; I have to be better and tougher than that.

One day, sit down and figure out what bothers you about your kids—the stuff that really makes you see red. If you can talk to a student who exhibits this trait, do it. Ask the kid to help you understand and deal with it appropriately. If this is not feasible, talk to a coworker, your department chair, or an administrator and ask for advice. Finally, brainstorm your own action plan and abide by it, making adjustments as you move along.

Questions for Reflection

1. How do you instill confidence in your students?

2. What do you do to make the subject you teach more relevant to your students' lives?

3. How do you encourage self-control in your students?

4. Think of students you've had whose preconceived notions about their capabilities affected their performance in class. What can a teacher do to change these notions?

5. What can a teacher do to promote behavior that is not always reinforced at home (e.g., organization, listening, self-control)?

6. How might you try to teach your students to react to behaviors and situations that bother them?

6

Underpinnings of a Caring Classroom

> *The difference between involvement and commitment is like ham and eggs. The chicken is involved; the pig is committed.*
>
> —Martina Navratilova

The more teachers understand their students, the more success they will have teaching those students. This relationship is a two-way street. If you care about your students, they know it, and they will come to care about you too. The more explicit you can be about your goals for the class, the better the students will respond to these goals.

Set the stage for managing your classroom with heart by committing to understand your students and helping them understand you. Help them understand how you devise the seating chart, derive their grades, and design class rules. The more they understand the inner workings of your teaching philosophy, the less room there will be for disdain and poor behavior.

Getting to Know Your Students

We think of our efficient teachers with a sense of recognition, but those who touched our humanity we remember with gratitude. Learning is the essential mineral, but warmth is the life-element for the child's soul, no less than for the growing plant.

—Carl Gustav Jung

My students sometimes confess that they feel "alone" in high school in a way that they never did in elementary school or middle school. Even though they are 14 or 16 or even 18 years old, they still need me, their teacher, to reach out to them: to find out who they are and tell them who I am and what they need to do to get along with me.

On the first day of school, after I've introduced myself, I tell the class they will be taking a test. On one hand, they're relieved to not have to sit through yet another account of classroom rules and expectations. (I save that talk for later in the first week, after class schedules have firmed up a bit.) On the other hand, they are incredulous: "A test on the first day of school?!" I assure them it's a test they can't fail.

I then explain and distribute a test designed to identify student learning styles: whether they are visual, auditory, or kinesthetic learners. (There are various tests like this available online; ask your school's guidance counselor for recommendations.) I let students know that the test results will tell them interesting things about themselves *and* help me be a better teacher for them. I also mention that I'll be using the test results to organize the classroom, and I announce that they'll be taking the test, figuring out their learning style, and receiving a description of their learning style all in one class period. This speech sends many messages that I don't explicitly verbalize:

- I care enough about them to find out about how they learn best.
- There will be a seating chart.
- I expect them to perform multiple tasks in one class period.

A working knowledge of my students' learning styles helps me devise more effective lesson plans and instructional approaches.

For example, if I know the majority of my third period students are visual learners, I am sure to make a written copy of the directions available. If I know that I have lots of kinesthetic learners, I'll ask the class to copy the directions from the overhead, the chalkboard, or my voice. I also provide lessons that incorporate opportunities to build a model, paint a picture, or sculpt a rendition.

On the first day of class, my students always get right to work on the learning style assessment. When they have finished and have asked me follow-up questions about their learning style, I ask them to fill out an index card with the following information:

1. Given name
2. Preferred name
3. Parent's or guardian's name and relationship to the student
4. Full address
5. Phone number
6. Learning style
7. Hobbies or interests

These pieces of information become a link between the student and me.

A note about "preferred names": Sometimes, I am not comfortable calling a student by his or her preferred name, and when this is the case, I say so. I had a student whose nickname was Peanut. I told him that I was afraid that he would think that I thought of him as less of a person if I called him that name, and he accepted this explanation. Then there was the girl who wanted me to call her Lady. All I could think of was the movie *Lady and the Tramp*. I told her that I naturally associated "Lady" with a dog and would rather have a more positive association with her name. At first she was resistant, but she grew used to being called by her given name and it was not an issue between us.

During the first couple of days, I allow students to sit wherever they like and note if they have friends in the class, who their friends are, and how they behave with or without friends. When I plan the seating chart, this information factors in my decisions. Generally, I put visual learners in the front, auditory learners in the back, and kinesthetic learners along the sides. If the students have shown me that they can work well sitting near their friends, I keep friends together. Friends who distract one another, however, I seat where they won't have easy eye contact.

Soon, the students begin describing themselves using their learning style preference. For example, a girl might say, "This is hard for me because I am visual, and you only gave the directions by speaking. Would you please write the directions on the board?" To this, I would reply that it's great that she recognizes her learning style, but she needs to learn to function in an environment that might not always be her ideal. Then I address her request: "No, I will not write the directions on the board, but I will repeat them slowly so you can take notes and *make* the directions visual."

I want students to see their learning styles as a reflection of the situation in which they learn best. I do *not* want them to use their learning styles as a crutch or a source of excuses ("He's a visual teacher and I'm a kinesthetic learner, so no wonder I'm failing."). One of a teacher's challenges is to help students learn how to adapt to their environment instead of insisting that the environment adapt to them. The former trains them for all kinds of future success; the latter just sets them up for failure.

Sharing behavioral guidelines and consequences

In general, once a teacher and the students understand one another, they can get on with the business of learning much more quickly. During the first week of school, I print my general list of classroom guidelines and the consequences for positive and negative behavior, and I go over this information with each of my classes. It's a list we'll refer to consistently throughout the year, and it goes like this:

1. Think before you speak or act.
2. Accept responsibility for your words and actions.
3. Set high expectations for your teacher and for yourself.

I also explain the consequences of bad behavior, sharing the four-step process (see Chapter 3). Then I talk about the consequences of good behavior: nonverbal recognition, verbal recognition, and a phone call home so that I can tell their parents how great they are.

Sharing pet peeves and making special accommodations

When I'm being upfront about the expectations I have for my students' behavior, I also tell them about my pet peeves (e.g., students talking while I am talking, interruptions, and messiness) and give them the opportunity to share expectations and pet peeves with me in a letter. I review each letter, making notes and seeing where I might accommodate the students. For example, I always honor requests for advance notice on reading assignments. And those who have good reasons for requesting special seating arrangements (e.g., they are prone to distraction and need to sit up front; their longtime enemy is in the class and they need to be separated) will generally get it. A request for "no homework" is an example of one I can't honor, but I do promise that I will only assign homework when it is necessary to extend a lesson; it will never be punishment or busywork. In this way, the students and I build connections and trust.

Marshalling Your Own Confidence

You gain strength, courage and confidence by every experience in which you really stop to look fear in the face. . . . You must do the thing you cannot do.

—Eleanor Roosevelt

When a teacher lacks confidence in any aspect of the job, the students *just know.* They know who is open to negotiation on the issue of a higher grade, who will let them argue about how a lesson should be completed, and who they can manipulate into letting them eat in class, arrive late, or leave early. A teacher's confidence comes with belief in the system he or she has designed and implemented. If you simply open the door on the first day of school and try to figure out a system as the days and weeks move along, the students will sense this, and they will feel that they have the right to teach you how to manage your classroom. But if you start with guidelines and you stick with them, the kids will know that you are in charge.

After you have stated your expectations, it's time to work on establishing your repertoire. How will the kids know when to get quiet? How will they know when it's OK to talk and be rowdy? How will the kids know when you are disciplining them? How will they be able to tell when you are being silly or being serious? Know the answers to these questions before the students set foot in the classroom and respond consistently throughout the year.

Also think about how you speak in the classroom. If necessary, work to refine your speech patterns by avoiding passive or vague language that might lead students to perceive you as unprepared, nervous, or ignorant. A statement such as "Today, I think we'll talk about the fall of the Roman Empire" tells kids that maybe you could be persuaded to talk about something else. Cut out the "I think," and just say, "Today, we will talk about the fall of the Roman Empire." This tells the kids that you have a plan and here it is.

Another habit that weakens a teacher's speech is the unconscious use of the question "OK?" ("Let's get out our books, OK?"). Do you actually want students' opinion on whether or why to get out those books? Losing the "OK?" makes you more likely to get students' cooperation and less likely to encounter resistance.

Some teachers cower at the thought of confronting students about misbehavior or grades. It is easier to overlook the student running in the hall or to give that student an *A* when he deserves a *B*. Students pick up on this quickly and don't hesitate to take advantage of it. It's a weakness that teachers must overcome; and although it's difficult, it's definitely possible.

The first thing I do when I recognize my own discomfort handling particular kinds of situations is to work on controlling my reactions. For example, it used to be difficult for me to simply tell a student no without also offering an explanation. I would feel compelled to explain *why* he could not go to the bathroom right then or *why* she could not have an extension on an assignment. I noticed that once

I started offering an explanation for my answers, the student would offer an explanation of his own. Back and forth we would go. I was wasting precious class time and losing my position as the classroom leader. To break this habit, I decided on a planned reaction: I would just say no, and if the student questioned me, I'd add, "You asked a question. I answered it. If you'd like a full discussion, come talk to me before or after school." I've found that this approach usually stops any arguing.

What interactions with students make you uncomfortable? Identify them and create a planned reaction. Perhaps you struggle with refusing to accept late work. Yes, you know the student is taking advantage of you, but you would really like to see this child succeed and so you give in. Take the time to devise a strategy to stop this student from taking advantage of your goodwill. Perhaps set up a one-on-one conference and explain that you will not be accepting late homework anymore, but you are here to help him develop strategies to get his homework in on time. From that point on, remain firm when he attempts to hand in homework late; he will either learn the lesson or not. It's called responsibility.

Yes, it will be difficult to implement your "planned reaction" at first, but once you do it a few times your confidence will soar, and you will be able to approach other challenging areas of the job with renewed vigor.

Assessing Multiple Components of Understanding

Imagination is more important than knowledge.
—Albert Einstein

In all subjects, there are assignments that are difficult to assign a grade to. In English class, papers fall into that category. My solution has been to give two grades: one for how well the student develops his or her thesis and the overall creativity of the essay and another for technical aspects, such as spelling, grammar, placement of thesis statement, and formatting of quotations and citations. This way, I do not penalize a poor speller with good ideas any more than I penalize a good speller with weak ideas.

Let's talk about spelling for a moment. I do not spend a lot of time working with spelling because when students enter the workforce as adults, they will have access to spell-checkers and dictionaries. What they won't have access to are "idea developers." Although teachers should point out errors and encourage students to work on troublesome words, we need to take seriously our responsibility to nurture students' creative thinking along with their technical proficiencies.

I use students' questions to help me assess both their understanding of the topic and their understanding of grammar. I encourage them to speak in correct English *and* to answer questions in a manner that reflects their understanding of the question. If I pay attention to their speech, I will hear where the gaps are in their understanding of both grammar and the topic. Written assignments also provide evidence of understanding in both areas. I note problems in a running list I maintain so that I can plan a future lesson that addresses the fact that they don't seem to understand how to write effective topic sentences or to logically present an argument.

In contrast, when it's difficult to explain to students *why* they need to understand certain curriculum-mandated grammatical concepts, they tend to perform miserably. For example, when I taught a week's worth of lessons on direct objects, indirect objects, and predicate nominatives, my students shut down after the second or third day. "This is to teach you whether or not your verbs take objects or not," I explained weakly. "But we know this already," they replied. And, in fact, 90 percent of the time, they *were* able to perform this skill, but it was the other 10 percent that I was trying to fix. Students telling me that they already knew what to do prompted me to find another way of approaching the topic. I sat down and identified verbs that do not take objects that they mistakenly put objects with. Then I taught these verbs specifically. Finally students could grasp the usefulness of this exercise. My first attempt at teaching them to fix their mistake was too abstract and misled them into thinking that they were doing something wrong that they were actually doing correctly. They needed a direct lesson, and that is what the second approach provided.

I realize that there are some things that students simply have to learn to be "educated" people who can pass the end-of-course test and interact well with other "educated" people. When these subjects come up, be honest: "This lesson involves material that you need to know, but it doesn't have any immediate relevance to your life beyond the fact that it will be on your test. When you are older and you are mixing with other educated people, you will be able to contribute to the conversation because you know this." I like to challenge my students to find a link between the lesson and their life. When they do come up with a connection, we discuss it and try to make it as relevant to every other student as possible.

Teenagers appreciate honesty and can sniff out a fake faster than any bloodhound. A fake tries to teach something without understanding its pertinence. Don't be a fake. Students are much more willing to cooperate with the lesson when you're honest about its purpose than when you have the attitude of "I'm teaching it, and you have no right to question why I'm teaching it." This kind of defensiveness gives the students justification to "check out" mentally. Students might learn enough to pass a test, but they will not connect with the lesson or incorporate new knowledge into their life.

Making Grades Make Sense

The most beautiful thing we can experience is the mysterious.
—Albert Einstein

When I was a student, I was conscientious about keeping track of my grades, and when report cards came out, I didn't have any surprises. When I became a teacher, I was surprised to discover how many of my students were completed astounded by what they saw on their report card. To remove the mystery surrounding grades and to minimize student confusion and gripe sessions, I now sit down with every student at the end of each quarter and give one- to two-minute "grade briefings" before report cards come out.

With a little advance planning, this is easy to manage. I start the class period with an explanation of the lesson for the day, which I design to incorporate independent work. I announce that as long as they are doing their work, I will be able to give everyone their grades and point out some places where improvement is needed or where their work is particularly excellent. I have never had a class become disruptive during this time.

To do this, set up a conference station in the back of the classroom. This will allow you to talk quietly to one student at a time but still monitor the rest of the class. Call students back in alphabetical order, show each his or her quarter grade, and explain how it was calculated. In my classes, I assign standard point values to various types of assignments. However, reciting this information ("As you may remember, Kelly, essays make up 25 percent of your grade . . .") will not necessarily make an impression. Instead, I might show Kelly, who aced the tests but failed to turn in any essays, the zeroes I've recorded for her in the essay spaces in my grade book. I then calculate what her grade would have been if she'd turned in the essays and received *D*s on them. Now it's easier for her to understand the impact of a zero and what she stands to lose when she chooses not to complete future essay assignments.

After discussing the grade, ask each struggling student to think about what is holding him or her back from excelling. If a student can name the problem, ask him to make a commitment to solving the problem and explain that the next time the two of you sit down together to talk about grades, you should be able to see some improvement in that problem area. Note that if there isn't any improvement, you reserve the right to question the steps he took to address the problem so that you two can discuss them together and come up with new steps that will help him achieve his goal.

The Importance of an Informative Grade Book

Every time we say "Let there be!" in any form, something happens.
—Stella Terrill Mann

A teacher's grade book is a mysterious thing to most students. They want to understand how their grades are calculated. My students like to come up and see their grades in the grade book and have me explain them. Although I want my students to understand their grades, we cannot spend a lot of time on any individual person's business during class time. I remind them of my tutoring hours before and after school if they want to have a long discussion. However, if we have a few minutes at the end of class, I will allow one student at a time come up and see his or her grades.

A well-organized grade book serves your students as well as it serves you. This truth was driven home by comments in a closing letter written to me by a student named Pauletta. She wrote that her history teacher "is unorganized. I don't even think she has a grade book. When you ask to see your grades, she won't show them to you because she doesn't know them." Pauletta was unsure if her efforts were even being recorded. She had no idea if she was passing or failing. Did she need to work harder? Where did she stand?

Seeing records of their grades helps students gauge whether or not they are doing well. For those who are struggling, seeing grades is often a good motivator. They can see their strengths and weaknesses, which helps them zero in on the specific problem instead of generalizing that their poor grade simply means that they are "bad" in English. For those whose work is average, it clarifies that there is room for improvement. The absence of a gauge is just one thing a student might use as an excuse to check out of class. As teachers, we should be working to eliminate as many of these potential excuses as we can.

A grade book must also serve the needs of the person who will be carrying it around for at least 180 days—you! Make it easy to figure grades and match the grades to particular assignments. Here are a couple of tips, based on what works for me.

- *Decide on your categories in your grade book.* These could include homework, quizzes, tests, projects, and class participation. Decide if you need another category for midterm and final exams, and decide the weight of each category.
- If it's an option for you, *take advantage of your school's network grade book.* These programs take the headache out of figuring each grade, calculating exams as 25 percent of the grade, homework as 10 percent, and so on. However, always keep a written record as a backup in case the mainframe crashes or some other glitch occurs.
- When you set up the actual grade book, *create one page exactly as you would like it to look.* This will serve as your template, ensuring that each class period's page looks the same and you can easily record grades without hunting around for sections. You will be moving quickly when you are recording your grades. You will want second period's homework section to be in the same place as third period's homework section.
- *Remember to plan ahead.* If you are in a school that follows a traditional time line, where students are in the same class for four quarters, give each class four pages in a row. This way, as you move through the year, each class has its own set of pages that are together and will be easy to maneuver within. You won't have to flip through the grade book to find third period's second-quarter grades because you will know exactly where they are.

You Are the Company You Keep

> *Keep away from people who belittle your ambitions. Small people always do that, but the really great make you feel that you too can become great.*
>
> —Mark Twain

When I first started teaching, I ate lunch with a crowd of teachers. I like to unwind a little bit in the middle of the day, and I thought eating with my colleagues would help me do that. I found that we usually talked about students and came to the general consensus that they were a pain. A few of the teachers asked for advice on issues, and I eagerly shared some of the methods that I had successfully employed.

As the weeks went on, I kept yammering away with advice and they kept complaining. Instead of trying out these ideas and experiencing some of the success I had, they began referring to me as the "lucky" teacher who had been assigned the "good" kids. Or I was "aggressive" and they were not. They said they could not do what I do. Well, I knew they were wrong. They said they had tried "everything" to reach their students, but what they really did was seek confirmation that the kids in their classes were indeed the "bad" and the "stupid" ones. And they expected these students to take 10 steps toward them while they just held the measuring stick and did nothing themselves.

I won't pretend I've never harbored feelings of frustration about my students, and these negative conversations brought out the worst of these feelings. Eventually, I realized this and stopped eating lunch with these teachers. Instead, I graded papers, met with students, or designed lesson plans. I no longer heard their lamentations about how they wished the kids would just be good, or just follow the rules, or just come to school.

How I decided to spend my lunch hour may seem like a rather petty topic, but it helped me hone in on a truth: We have choices to make, and if we don't make them, someone will make them for us. These teachers were choosing for me whether I was going to be happy with my work and with my students or unhappy with them. I took my choice back. And I'm a happier person and a more effective teacher because of it.

Noninstructional Duties

You will do foolish things, but do them with enthusiasm.

—Colette

In order to run a school, the principal relies on the help of the faculty. It often comes as a surprise to newer teachers who may be asked to substitute for another teacher or even to monitor the bus lot. These can be stressful jobs simply because it means running into students you do not know and yet will need to manage. Be prepared for them to test your limits.

More frequently than I would like, when I step in as an emergency substitute, there aren't any lesson plans waiting for me. I've learned to show up with crossword puzzles or something similar so I am certain to have something that will occupy the students. Busy students are generally cooperative students, so I bring the busywork. If they have nothing to do, they will start thinking of things to do: go to the bathroom, get some water, or go to their cars. They will "need" to call home or paint their nails. The activities I have are not necessarily the most mindful or educational, but I am at least making an effort to create a peaceful environment.

If there is a lesson plan left behind, I follow it. I make sure to read the directions to the students and write the directions on the board. I monitor the students as if they were my own and take notes on general class participation and particular individual inattention, although I do ease up on the "no talking" rule and just make sure the talking does not get out of hand. I also stick to my standard discipline steps of a nonverbal warning followed by a verbal warning and a discussion in the hallway, but if a student fails to comply after that, I don't hesitate to call security and have that student removed. The less I allow a student to be disrespectful, the more smoothly that class period will go. The other students will watch to see where my "line" is. If it looks as though I'm willing to let students walk all over me, many will try to do it. But if I make it clear that I won't be walked on, most will not attempt it.

These noninstructional duties are not what most educators have in mind when they sign their teaching contract, but they are nonetheless part of the job. Always know the laws in your state and the job descriptions in your contract involving planning periods, breaks, and lunch periods. It is your responsibility to make sure you are not being taken advantage of. Do not entrust this responsibility to anybody else.

Hugging Students

The meeting of two personalities is like the contact of two chemical substances: if there is any reaction, both are transformed.
—Carl Gustav Jung

Babies who are not held or touched by their parents fail to thrive. Many students are failing to thrive for that very same reason. No one gives them the hugs, the hand holding, or the shoulder squeezes that send the message, "You are OK."

Yes, physical contact with students is a very sensitive issue because of perceptions of impropriety and, sad to say, students' awareness that they could twist a simple hug into a sexual encounter and then call that teacher's professionalism into question. Acknowledging this, I remain "pro-hug." In fact, I had a student, Arisha, who always said hello to me at the door each day and gave me a hug. She seemed to need that from me, and to be honest, it was nice to know that I would encounter at least one caring person each day. Still, when it comes to touching students, I am very careful to respect their boundaries and let them know where my boundaries are.

I handle boys differently from the way I handle girls. I never want to confuse a teenage boy about the kind of caring I feel for him. My interest in him is as a person and as a student, but decidedly not as a romantic partner. I tend to give boys arm-over-the-shoulder-type hugs. It keeps our relationship on clear footing. I shake hands with them when I want to "close a deal" on their behavior. I will squeeze a shoulder when I want to wake them up or get their attention. Sometimes I will gently poke them in the ribs with my pencil when they are fooling around in class. Their own giggles and comments of "OK, OK" get them back on task.

If I am alone with a student, whether that student is male or female, I leave the classroom door open and send clear body language that I am available to listen and discuss personal concerns, but our relationship is a teacher-student one. This body language includes standing or sitting one foot or more away from the student, looking into the student's eyes, and maintaining formal, upright posture throughout the discussion. I also am careful to keep my voice calm and even throughout the conversation and remember the four guidelines.

Now, some frank talk: I once watched as a colleague of mine confused her role as a teacher with her role as a friend to the students. She did not discourage the boys from hugging her in what appeared to me to be a very sexual manner. When I asked her if this made her uncomfortable, she said that it did, a little, but she did not want her students to dislike her.

There is a fine line between appropriate and inappropriate physical contact with students. However, you do not help anybody by becoming a cold person who backs away from a student who needs a hug. The student receives the message "I do not care about you," and you are allowing fear to control you. Instead, show the student that you care and give an appropriate hug.

The Rise and Fall of Student Effort

Nobody sees a flower—really—it is so small it takes time— we haven't time—and to see takes time, like to have a friend takes time.
—Georgia O'Keeffe

The roughest quarter of the year is first quarter. I am just beginning to "see" my students and they are just beginning to "see" me. If I set up guidelines and consistently follow them, then second quarter will go smoothly. Students will understand that my actions are not arbitrary and my assignments are purposeful. My reaction to disciplinary concerns is timely, fair, and reasonable, and my interactions with the students are sincere. Kids respond to these behaviors.

Second quarter usually moves smoothly. By third quarter, many students slack off and take home lower grades than they do all year. By fourth quarter, they are with me 100 percent. They know what it takes to pass, and they trust me enough to help them when they are struggling. They are confident that I will provide and maintain an atmosphere that is conducive to learning. It is nice to see students who are relaxed enough in class to enjoy themselves. They actually want to be in class, and they want to succeed.

I save the most challenging work for fourth quarter because it's then that my students are the most ready academically and behaviorally. As the year comes to a close, I find myself lamenting the fact that I will never teach the same sets of kids again. I start watching their every gesture and listening to their every word. I am putting these things in my long-term storage. I want to remember these people.

Questions for Reflection

1. What message would you like to convey to your students on the first day of school?

2. What steps might you take to ensure that your intended message is being conveyed?

3. What are your pet peeves?

4. How do your students perceive your level of confidence?

5. How do you inform students of their grades?

6. Does your grade book have room for improvement? If so, in what areas?

7. How do you feel about hugging your students?

7

It's the Little Things That Can Throw Off Your Day

To be really great in little things, to be truly noble and heroic in the insipid details of everyday life, is a virtue so rare as to be worthy of canonization.
—Harriet Beecher Stowe

It's the little things that make life sweet. I think about holding my husband's hand for the first time, about crossing a half-marathon finish line with my sister, about wiping away tears as my son happily boarded the school bus, and about seeing a student's eyes light up when he grasps a new concept. I'm not going to talk about those things in this chapter. Instead, I want to talk about those things that can throw a teacher off, catch you unprepared, and make you feel as though you have chosen the wrong profession. They are the things that can ruin your entire day, but only if you let them.

It should be no surprise that the approach to various responsibilities and components of classroom life presented in this chapter is informed by the four guidelines for interacting with students. I've learned that if I am true to those guidelines and (1) don't let students fast-talk me, (2) stay focused on the problem, (3) see the big picture, and (4) don't sell out my values, I will be serving my students well. By handling the fine details of the job in a caring, considerate, and respectful manner, I work toward my ultimate goal of creating and maintaining a positive learning environment. You can do the same.

Getting Class Started

You are the bows from which your children as living arrows are sent forth.

—Kahlil Gibran

A bad beginning can sabotage the entire class period. It is easy to get caught up in the frenzy of bells ringing, students talking, and lockers slamming, but try to let the noise pass and focus on each class period with the same energy you used to design the day's lesson plan.

I have found that structuring a class in a certain manner gives students something to rely on and serves as a model of organization that I hope will help them organize the different segments of their lives. After the bell rings, I always walk into the classroom, say good morning, get my roll book, and quickly take attendance. This gives the students a few seconds to become settled, finish their conversations, and generally breathe the air of my classroom. After I finish taking attendance, I look around. If anyone is still talking, I look at them and wait. Generally, that is enough to end any conversation. If a student does not have his feet under his desk, I say, "OK, let's get swiveled." For some reason, this word, *swivel*, is very effective. I once heard a veteran teacher use it in her classroom, and it was a nonpunitive demand that was just silly enough to get the students to sit properly without getting mad. *(Guideline #4: Don't sell out your values.)* I've been using *swivel* ever since. Sometimes I'll just look at a student, and she will slide her feet under her desk, smiling and saying, "Swivel!"

"Swivel" has become my trademark. I've found that students like to associate something, an action or a word, with an authority figure.

The predictability helps to make the authority figure seem accessible because at least one facet of his or her personality is constant. This establishes a sort of common ground that helps the students relax and open up to the lessons.

If students are looking at each other, down at their shoes, or at a note on their desks, then they are not ready to start class. As I scan the room, I look for all eyes to be on me. When kids' eyes are elsewhere, I look at them until they look at me, or I ask them to put away whatever has their attention.

Sometimes a class is just pumped up, and more than one or two students are talking. When this happens, I say, "Are we ready?" Usually the students treat this as the rhetorical question that I mean it to be, and everyone swivels and stops talking. Of course, every once in a while a student will say, "No, I'm not ready." I just smile, and if that student smiles back, I know we can begin. If there's no smile, I gently say, "I see you're having a rough time getting started today. Please do your best to get ready while the rest of the class and I get started." Then I start class.

As I get to know my students better over the course of the year, I devise additional methods that are effective in getting particular students' attention. *(Guideline #2: Stay focused on the problem.)* I did this for Kelvin, the tough kid from New York. He loved shoes. Not only did he always seem to be wearing new shoes, he was constantly studying catalogs looking for his next pair. Once he mentioned to me how his dad was going to send him a pair of the new $150 Air Jordans. By sharing this little piece of information from his life, Kelvin gave me a tool I could use. As I was getting ready to begin class the next day, I spied the shoe catalog on Kelvin's desk. All I had to say was, "OK, Kelvin, I know you want to pick out your next new pair of shoes, but I need you to put the catalog away. Your dad will be mailing those Jordans sooner than you know." Sure enough, he put the catalog away. I showed him that I had listened to him tell me about his dad, and I acknowledged a practice that he respected—his father buying him his shoes. This was enough to persuade him to follow my request.

Daily Agendas, Directions, and Discussions

Discipline is the refining fire by which talent becomes ability.
—Roy L. Smith

After gaining students' attention, it is time to transition into the learning. This routine creates yet another connection between teacher and students. I begin by quickly summarizing the previous day's lesson and explaining what we will be doing today. This gives students a mental checklist to follow as we move through the class period. I find that when I add things to the list after I have started teaching, the students are less willing to accept them as legitimate exercises and more likely to see them as busywork. For this reason, I try to plan carefully and keep in mind how much time each part of the lesson will require so that I won't need to add new components on the spot. Of course, not every plan will be perfect; on those occasions when I must add an exercise, I do not accept the students' whining. I admit to misjudging the amount of time the day's lesson would take. I then say, "I am going to give you a head start on tomorrow's work," and begin the new exercise's explanation. By framing the "extra" work as an advantage to them, I appeal to their desire to be ahead of the game.

Once I reach a point where I must give the students directions for an assignment, it is tempting to simply give all the directions at once. When I do this with my younger students at the beginning of the year, the response is usually something like, "You want us to do *what?*" So I repeat the directions. Then the kids say, "OK, we get the first two parts, but what was the last part?" So I repeat the directions yet again and find myself becoming frustrated. I've learned that it's helpful to space out directions over time, as the students complete components of an assignment, or to provide instructions in writing, either on the board or on the worksheet. Many students can handle one direction very easily, but once I give them more than that, they begin to feel overwhelmed. Throughout the year, I increase the number of directions that I give at one time.

I keep this incremental approach in mind when I am posing questions during a class discussion. *(Guideline #3: See the big picture.)* I ask one question at a time, and I use a wait time of three to six seconds before calling on somebody. This may seem like a long wait, but it sends the message that both the question and the answer require thought and that thinking is a worthy way to use class time. The practice prompts deeper reflection from students whose minds work quickly and are used to blurting out answers, and it also expands the discussion to include the naturally deep thinkers whose contributions might go unheard in a rapid-fire exchange as well as students who process their thoughts more slowly and might otherwise not even bother to think about an answer.

What if a student's answer is off track, off topic, or just incorrect? If the student is off track, I will try to redirect him by bridging the gap of his understanding. For example, I teach a unit on slavery literature. During a discussion of the negro spiritual, which I was lauding as an uplifting form of expression, a student once commented, "So you think slavery was OK because these negro spirituals came out of slavery?"

A deep breath goes a long way in these scenarios. *(Guideline #2: Stay focused on the problem.)* I took one and then said, "What do you think, class? Should we still have slavery since we did get some negro spirituals out of it? Is it possible for good things to come out of terrible situations? Does this make the terrible situation 'worthwhile,' or do we need to think about the question in a different way?"

The idea in this specific situation was to step back from the personal challenge the student was presenting to me; the general idea is to encourage the student and his classmates to take a step back, take a broader view of the topic, and engage in some higher-level thinking.

If a question I ask has a clear right-or-wrong answer, I try to connect a student's incorrect response to a correct one. I restate the question with the student's first answer in mind and then wait for a response. Nobody likes to be shot down in front of peers, and teenagers take embarrassment especially hard. If I asked for the date of the Emancipation Proclamation and a student says, "1776," I will reassure him that he was thinking of a different relationship than slave and owner: "You're actually thinking of the year the United States became independent from the British Empire." The student saves face, I don't sell out my values *(Guideline #4),* and I am free to restate the question.

Many adolescents get into the habit of responding to direct questions with an "I don't know." Usually, what they really mean is "I don't care." I show them that *I* care by refusing to accept "I don't know" as an answer. I restate the question so that it's more thought provoking for the individual—perhaps by relating it to the student's life or using terms that are more familiar. For example, when I asked Dana why she thought slaves created negro spirituals, and she said, "I don't know," I prompted her with another question: "When do you sing, Dana?"

She paused and replied, "At church. And in the car, sometimes, with my sister. I don't know. In a lot of places."

I pushed a little further. "*Why* do you sing?"

"Ms. Ridnouer! 'Cause it's fun. I feel heard. I feel understood."

I continued pushing. "Dana, would you read the lyrics of 'This World Is Almost Done'?"

"OK. 'Brudder, keep your lamp trimmin' and a-burnin', Keep your lamp trimmin' and a-burnin', Keep your lamp trimmin' and a-burnin', For dis world most done. So keep your lamp trimmin' and a-burnin', Dis world most done."

"Thank you, Dana. Now why do you think the creator of this song sang it?"

"Well, I guess he wanted God to hear him because nobody on earth ever did."

Dana *did* know. And she was surprised to find that she cared too.

Finally, I encourage all students to ask questions about the question if they don't know the answer right off the bat. While teaching *The Catcher in the Rye,* I might say, "Holden Caulfield says that 'the best thing, though, in that museum was that everything always stayed right where it was. Nobody'd move . . . Nobody'd be different.'

Why do you think Holden felt this way about the Museum of Natural History?"

If blank stares follow, I might ask, "Any questions about the question?" I give it some wait time, maybe 10 or 20 seconds, before calling on someone: "Lasondra, where is Holden *supposed* to be at this point in the story?" This is a fact in the book that I know she knows.

"He's supposed to be at school, but he left early. He doesn't really know where he is going with his life. OK, I get it. Maybe being in the museum—somewhere where nothing changes—helps him feel calm."

Refocusing the question on a factual aspect of the novel—or on another concept or aspect of content they have mastered—helps students frame the context of the question. Because they are successful in understanding the reframed question, they are willing to try to answer the original one. This helps to build their confidence in the thinking tools that they already have.

Treacherous Transitions

One learns by doing the thing; for though you think you know it, you have no certainty until you try.

—Sophocles

The transition from one part of a lesson to the next is the time when students are most likely to misbehave. The reason many teachers experience chaos during transitions is because they are spending time looking for worksheets or page numbers or other things they should have found before class started. The students are left waiting, and idle students tend to get into more mischief than busy ones.

I make sure my students always have something to do, and steadfast organization is what makes this possible. First thing each morning, I read over my lesson plans and then pull out everything I will be using that day. I stack the worksheets, student work, and books on the corner of my desk in the order that I will need them. I do not lose the momentum of the first part of the lesson to move into the second or the third and so on. If I'm doing something that requires students to wait on me, I always give them a small task to occupy themselves. As I pass out worksheets, for example, I tell them to get out their writing utensil. They have no time to start conversations or engage in any other off-task behavior.

I insist on a fast pace in my classroom. This does not mean that I cut out time for questions or practice, but it does mean that I give my students an approximate amount of time I will allow for each exercise. I might say, "We have five minutes for questions. What is unclear?" Or I'll say, "You have 10 problems. You should easily be able to complete one problem every two minutes. I'll give you 20 minutes to complete this worksheet." I am telling them that I have a plan and high expectations for them. They usually respond well to this unless I've miscalculated their abilities or incorrectly gauged the difficulty of the material. In that case, they let me know, and I make suitable adjustments.

Wrapping Up a Lesson

Many ideas grow better when they are transplanted into another mind than the one where they sprang up.
—Oliver Wendell Holmes

At the end of each class, I summarize the day's lesson and tell students how we will use what we've learned that day in the lesson I have planned for the next day. This gives the students closure and an opportunity to ask any last-minute questions. I usually end class two or three minutes before the bell and permit students to talk during this time so they can relax a little bit before they have to get up and head into another class period full of study. *(Guideline #3: See the big picture.)* Two or three minutes, I've found, is just about right: enough time for the "chatty Kathies" to share what's new in their lives but not so much time that introverted students feel ashamed of sitting quietly or pressured to think of things to say. During this time, students are also free to ask me questions about an assignment or to let me know they will be absent the next day and get the work that they will miss. Following this model consistently makes students less likely to pack up prematurely and helps ensure that I will have their attention when I need it.

Paperwork: "Teacher Division"

In the middle of difficulty lies opportunity.

—Albert Einstein

Teachers receive what seems like thousands of pounds of paper throughout a school year. We expect each of our students to be organized, and it's hardly fair to ask this of them if we don't ask it of ourselves. Here's what I recommend: From day one, set up separate, alphabetical folders for all your "teacher stuff": department information, referrals and other documentation, general faculty information, committee paperwork, class rules and syllabi, the never-ending roster updates, the student handbook, and homeroom information.

These files can help even when you're not in the classroom. One day, while I was waiting in a long line to use the copier during my planning period, an administrator walked up and said, "Ms. Ridnouer, Tanya's mother is here. I need you to get her report card."

Had I just wasted 20 precious minutes of my planning period? No. Because of my filing system, I did not have to get out of line. I simply said, "If you don't mind walking to my classroom, the report card is in my homeroom folder that is in the file organizer on my desk. You'll find the file in alphabetical order." After I had made my copies, I returned to my classroom and checked my files. Sure enough, the administrator had found Tanya's report card with no problem. Everyone was happy.

I also recommend keeping a stacked tray-style organizer on your desk for items you continually check on, refer to, or revise. My receipt book stays in there, as do the lists of students who are going on field trips. A school schedule for a special event is in there, and so is an explanation of any new policies. Now, when a student tells me that she has to leave because the choir is performing at 12:30, I can check the choir director's memo to make sure the student is giving me accurate information. Being able to pull out documentation to back up my answer eliminates the possibility of an argument.

Finally, if your school is anything like mine, at the beginning of the year, you receive stacks of lists: a list of telephone extensions, the bell schedules for special days, a list of holidays, a list of school testing days, and so on. It's a good idea to keep all of these in the same place. During that first week of school, I take the time to tape each of these sheets to my desk so that it's there for easy reference when a student or I have a question. It's also very satisfying to peel away these sheets at the end of the school year.

Of course, a good deal of the paperwork a teacher must manage contains information that can also help keep students organized and on track. Although I keep original documents in my folder system, I post excerpts for all to see. For example, I print bell schedules and grading scales on brightly colored paper and hang them up around the room. I also post a copy of the county's graduation schedule, with our school highlighted. Even though I do not teach seniors, all of my students seem to glance at it every day. Posting this schedule serves as a nonverbal message to them that I am here to help them toward their end goal. *(Guideline #4: Don't sell out your values.)* They come to know that if one group of students can get to that graduation date, so can they.

Paperwork: "Student Division"

We first make our habits, and then our habits make us.
—John Dryden

Think of how many pieces of paper your students turn in to you over the course of a school year. I recommend a two-part organizational approach that will help you handle it all in a manner that benefits both the students and you.

A submission/return system for assignments

Set up a folder for each class period's assignments and keep them in a folder organizer in clear view. I keep mine on my desk as a visual reminder that I have papers to grade or graded assignments to distribute. It's significant that students see me using these folders to sort and manage my paperwork. Not only does this model good organization practices, it reassures students that I won't lose work that they submit and discourages them from using the "But I turned it in!" excuse. On the rare occasions when an assignment does "go lost," I give the student a day to find it with no penalty. *(Guideline #2: Stay focused on the problem.)* This saves instructional time, as there is no need for discussion, and gives me the opportunity to check if I *did* accidentally file the student's paper with work from another class. It also gives the student a chance to "redo" the assignment, which is what I really want anyway.

A system for long-term storage of significant work

Maintaining a separate portfolio-style system for certain assignments is an excellent way to track students' progress over the course of a year. As an English teacher, I maintain a writing folder for each of my students, where I file every writing assignment they complete.

It is a simple system to manage. I take a plastic milk crate, tape on a sign that reads "Writing Folders," turn five folders long-ways, and label each with a specific class period. Then I create an individual folder for each student and file it in the appropriate class folder. Each time I have a writing assignment to return, I either file the paper in each student's folder myself and hand out the folders, or pass out the folders and the papers at the same time. (It just depends on how much time I want to spend on this activity.) I give the students time to read my comments and corrections, and then they return the paper to the folder and hand it back to me to be filed in the class-specific folder. When they are at the editing stage of their next assignment, I pass out their writing folders again so they can look over their mistakes to be sure to not repeat them. This is especially helpful for my 11th graders, who must attend to all the particulars related to writing their first "real" research paper. Having an old paper to refer to helps jog their memory of what goes where.

Often, students want to bring their "first A paper" home, and I will let them, provided that they promise to bring it back and put it in their folder. When they do, they usually have a story to share about their parents' praise.

Why insist on keeping all the papers? To offset my high schoolers' sometimes less-than-stellar organizational skills. Many would be likely to lose or trash their essays and not blink an eye. Then, they would lose out on the impact of seeing the difference between August's essays and June's essays when I distribute fat folders full of writing to every student at the end of the school year. The first thing many of them say is, "Man, I did a lot of work this year!" Pride. After skimming through some of their earlier essays, some of them say, "I sure could not spell back then." Achievement. Then someone asks, "Now can I take this home?" Ownership.

Substitute Teachers

People are always good company when they are doing what they really enjoy.

—Samuel Butler

Leaving adolescent students in somebody else's hands for even one day is a scary proposition. Kids this age can be cruel to anyone they perceive as weak, stupid, or some other adjective they feel will justify misbehavior. It is each teacher's responsibility to help his or her students be good company for the substitute teacher. Here are some guidelines that help ensure positive substitute experiences.

Prepare your students. If possible, let your kids know a day in advance that you will be absent. (Any more notice might prompt them to conceive of a "battle plan.") Go over the lesson plan for that day and explain how you will handle discipline concerns. I always tell my students that I know they will treat the substitute in the same fine manner that they treat me. Then I provide the substitute with a handy sheet to fill out if any of my students do not comply with my request.

Try to hand-pick your substitute. You can get to know who the good substitutes are simply by listening and being observant. Does security seem show up every period when Mr. Smith is subbing for the class next door? Perhaps he is too strict or tends to overreact. Do students seem to be constantly coming and going from the class Ms. Jones is subbing for across the hall? Perhaps she is too lenient. Get to know the substitutes by introducing yourself when you see them in a colleague's room. Listen, with a grain of salt, to what the kids have to say. Choose your substitute with all this information in mind. My substitute of choice is a retired teacher who is quiet, firm, and loving, and I will "book her" up to a month in advance. The kids say they "just can't be mean to her."

Be sure to prepare both the substitute and the lesson. This means remembering to make a copy of attendance rosters and leave the substitute the names and room numbers of teachers to go to for help. And it means double-checking that you have typed up or printed out the lesson plan for each class you teach and have also provided backup assignments. I'll often treat the days with a substitute teacher as review days. I will make up a worksheet that the students can fill out with the help of their notes and the textbook, and I provide the substitute with an answer key complete with page references to help students find the answers. I'll ask the substitute to review the worksheet at the end of class and collect the students' work so that I can see what went on in my absence. I will also leave word games and word puzzles for the students to complete if they finish early. It's important that this be high-interest material, so the students will want to do it instead of seeking other forms of entertainment, such as disrupting class.

Finally, even if you are confident you've chosen a good substitute, it's a good idea to lock up anything that you do not want to "walk away" in your absence. I always lock my desk and leave the substitute a clearly marked folder containing the lesson plans, the student rosters and seating charts, the names of the teachers standing by to help, referral forms, attendance cards, pens and pencils, a spare textbook, and extra notebook paper. This approach keeps all the material in one place, the substitute prepared, and your property secure.

It is a wonderful thing to return from a day off and read glowing reports about each of your classes. Some of the reports I get glow more brightly than others, but all of them are usually positive. I read each class their report and thank them for their cooperation. They are justly proud of themselves: high school students who have not only behaved but actually *learned something* with a substitute leading the class.

Textbook Management

Few things can help an individual more than to place responsibility on him, and to let him know that you trust him.
—Booker T. Washington

Replacing lost and damaged textbooks costs schools thousands of dollars each year. It is the classroom teacher's responsibility to ensure that these textbooks are distributed in such a way that the students will have access to books when necessary and will be held responsible for the books' undamaged return at the end of the year. After a few years of trying to pass out textbooks quickly and not so efficiently, I have opted for a slower, more efficient routine that you might consider trying.

At the beginning of the school year, I design a lesson that the students can complete on their own while I distribute the books one at a time. I sign the inside front cover of the book, note the general condition of the book, and write in the student's name. I then have the student sign a sheet that records the book number and the date the student signed out the book. This way I have a record of everyone receiving a book and the number of the book received. At the end of the year, there is no question about whether or not this student or that student owes me a book; I can simply return to the list and see if the student has signed in the book. If he has not, he owes the school some money.

Another common problem with textbooks is that once the students have received them, they are not always willing to bring them back to class when they need them. If students know that the only punishment they will receive for failing to bring their books is a sigh and an eye roll from the teacher, putting out the extra effort to bring a book to class doesn't make sense to them. Those students who do bring their books consistently will not feel good about continuing the practice if their teacher doesn't hold accountable those students who do not. Each teacher must come up with a system that works to keep frustration at bay for the teacher, the compliant student, and the noncompliant student.

One system that works for me was passed on to me by my department chair, Angela Brathwaite. I ask the students to raise their hands if they would like an automatic "100" for a test grade. Invariably, all but a few suspicious students eagerly raise their hands. I say, "Fine. You all have a 100 in the grade book at this moment." Then I pause.

"What's the catch?" they ask.

"Oh, you want to know what this grade is for? OK. Every day that you are to bring your textbook to class, I will conduct a quick book check. If you have your book, you get to keep your 100. If you don't, you lose 10 points. Can you guess what happens if you forget to bring your book twice?"

A student will usually call out, "You lose another 10 points and get an 80 for the test grade."

"Exactly. That's a *C,* but it could've been an *A.* What if you forget your book 10 times?"

Nobody likes the sound of this question, but someone always answers: "You have a zero for a test grade."

"Exactly. I will average that zero with your other test grades, and it will definitely ruin a good average. I want you to understand that if you expect to pass your classes, you *must* be prepared. Bringing your book every day is one way you can be prepared. What are some other ways?"

I segue into a short discussion about bringing paper, pen, and pencil along with homework, and a rested and fed body. In this way, I tell my students what my expectations are and why they should want to meet those expectations.

If you set up a system like this, plan to field some questions about how that system will work:

Student: OK, so if we do not bring our book, then do we just sit here with 10 points gone and no book?

Teacher: That's a good question. You seem to be concerned about whether you will be penalized twice for the same offense. Am I right? *(Guideline #2: Stay focused on the problem.)*

Student: Yeah. That would stink. I hate sitting here without a book just having to listen.

Teacher: I agree. That can be boring. What I will do is take off the points for those of you who don't have your books and then lend you a book for the period. How does that sound? *(Guideline #4: Don't sell out your values.)*

Student: Fair enough.

In my system, students start every quarter with that 100 percent, so they have 4 opportunities a year to take advantage of a free perfect test score. An alternative approach might be to check for books randomly 10 times each quarter and award 10 points each time to those who have them. As each quarter begins, I make a big deal about letting them know that it's a good time to begin bringing their books if they are not already in the habit of doing so. Many students don't need this extra cheerleading, but there are always a few who do. In the end, the book grade serves as a bonus to conscientious students (usually the majority of the class) when I average their quarter grades. Along the way, they feel validated for doing what is right, and I experience fewer frustrating incidents of students showing up in class without the book they need.

Bathroom Passes

People's minds are changed through observation and not through argument.

—Will Rogers

A trip to the bathroom provides a perfect way for students to escape a boring lecture or those cramp-inducing desks. As teachers, we can't know if a student really has to go, and we cannot accompany them. Many of us let students leave class for a bathroom break whenever they ask and are left hoping they do not take advantage of our trust. Other teachers do not allow students out of the room under any circumstances.

If you aren't comfortable with either of these choices, consider a middle ground. Here is what I say to my students: "I expect you to come to class to stay for all 48 minutes of it. I do understand that emergencies arise; therefore, I have developed a system for giving out bathroom passes. You have one bathroom pass each quarter. You may use it at any time during the quarter, but once you've used it, that's it for the rest of the quarter. Plan ahead and you'll be fine. In the past, I have taught students who had bladder problems, and I allotted them more than one emergency a quarter. If you have such a concern, just bring in a doctor's note, and I'll be happy to release you as needed."

At first the students find this to be unreasonable, and they do not believe that I will enforce the policy. They become believers when they see me making a notation in my grade book each time I give out a bathroom pass, or when they hear me say, "No, you may not go to the bathroom. You have already used your emergency pass." They realize that I value class time, and they stop dreaming up escape routes. They have no reason to argue with me, and we can easily get back to the lesson.

Should you allow exceptions? I do, occasionally. *(Guideline #3: See the big picture.)* I had one student who needed to cross the entire campus to get to my class and barely had time to make it. At my school, we are not allowed to release students during the first or last 10 minutes of class, so she learned to ask me if she could use the bathroom after the first 10 minutes. She was so discrete exiting and reentering the classroom that the other students did not seem to notice her absence. She also waited for an opportune moment to get work that she might have missed. The system forced her to refine her manners in order to earn the special exception she desperately needed.

Homework Assignments

When you get into a tight place and everything goes against you until it seems that you cannot hold on for a minute longer, never give up then, for that is just the place and time that the tide will turn.

—Harriet Beecher Stowe

I maintain a homework board, which consists of four index cards that I've enlarged to poster size and laminated. I tape these to the wall so that they form a huge square. Every morning, I use an overhead pen to record the day's date and upcoming homework assignment for each of my classes. Because the board is laminated, it's easy to maintain; I simply wipe off the older dates and assignments as I need space.

The homework board accomplishes many things:

• When students walk into class, they can see immediately if they have homework that night. They know that any homework I will give is a planned part of the lesson. It is not a punishment. They can also gauge how much work time they will have to put in that night. There are no surprises.

• Those who have been absent will find a record of up to two weeks of missed homework assignments.

• When administrators or parents come in the room, they too have a visual record of the assigned homework for that day and the previous two weeks.

- Because it is situated where I can read it standing in front of the room, I can reference the page numbers and other information without having to refer to my planning book.
- It becomes the student's responsibility to get homework assignments, not mine. This helps to teach self-reliance.

Reading Assignments

If he is indeed wise he does not bid you enter the house of wisdom, but rather leads you to the threshold of your own mind.
—Kahlil Gibran

I teach English, and reading novels is a big part of what we do. I have found that my students like to know what we are going to read and when we are going to read it. For each book assigned, I make up a pacing chart, organized by week and including dates, pages to read, and vocabulary words to define. Figure 2 (p. 128) shows a sample pacing chart. Using a spreadsheet program simplifies the process because I can get a lot of information onto a 4″ × 5″ sheet, which the students can easily use as a bookmark.

My students can use the information in the pacing chart to plan their week, or they can ignore it. It is their choice. I have made no value judgment about their choice, and the students get to maintain ownership of their decision.

The students invariably know when a night of "lots of reading" is coming up because they have looked at their pacing charts. They also know that if we are reading the book together and they settle in quickly, we will have more time to read the pages in class and they will have less homework. Everyone wins.

These pacing charts are great for a population such as the one I teach, where attendance is inconsistent. A student might be out of school, but he knows what the assignment is, and if he chooses to keep up with the class, he can easily do so.

Figure 2
Sample Pacing Chart

Incidents in the Life of a Slave Girl
by Harriet Jacobs

Vocabulary and Readings

Week of JAN 19

M HOLIDAY	1. mulatto	7. defraud	13. chattel
T pp. 11–43	2. maternal	8. epicure	14. toil
W pp. 44–70	3. diligent	9. conjecture	15. vile
Th pp. 71–96	4. blasphemy	10. balsam	16. bondage
F pp. 97–121	5. detain	11. dint	17. retrospect
	6. candelabra	12. corporal	18. vigilant

Week of JAN 26

M pp. 122–144	19. malevolence	25. bough	31. blight
T pp. 145–166	20. contempt	26. entreat	32. extremity
W pp. 167–178	21. clime	27. manumit	33. avowal
Th pp. 179–192	22. vex	28. pervade	34. chafe
F pp. 193–223	23. emigrate	29. submission	35. wrought
	24. interment	30. retribution	36. tinge

Week of FEB 2

M pp. 224–248	37. dissention	43. rebuke	49. prattle
T pp. 249–263	38. renounce	44. consternation	50. constable
W pp. 264–278	39. infernal	45. remonstrate	51. gratification
Th pp. 279–295	40. venomous	46. induce	52. conjecture
F pp. 296–303	41. lacerate	47. provocation	53. procure
	42. epithet	48. vocation	54. interstices

Project Assignments

One worthwhile task carried to a successful conclusion is worth half a hundred half-finished tasks.

—B. C. Forbes

When the class is completing an extended project, such as a research paper, I create and distribute a project organizer for students to keep in their notebooks and refer to throughout the term of the project. I've found that if I treat each part of the project as an assignment with a grade, the project as a whole becomes much more manageable for the students. They see it not as one big, daunting leap, but as a collection of small steps. As shown in the sample organizer in Figure 3 (pp. 130–131), I include due dates in bold print, a full explanation and the point value of each component assignment, and references to additional materials students might need.

Although creating project organizers takes advance planning and development work, it ends up saving time in the long run. There aren't any daily arguments about what should be done when because it's all written out. For some reason, the written word is very powerful to students—much more powerful than the spoken word. For the same reason, it's more effective for me to use a written project organizer to *show* my students that a project is a series of manageable steps than it is for me to *tell* them the same thing. By seeing the steps and doing the work, they discover the truth of this for themselves.

The project organizer gives the students many choices. They can do some of the assignments, all of the assignments, or none of them because each part receives a grade. It's their choice. Certainly I can remind them, take points off for late work, and refuse to accept work after a given time period. These are all preset conditions. Although there are choices to be made, there is nothing to discuss: nothing for the student, the parent, the administrator, the counselor, or you, the teacher, to react negatively to. This teaches the student how to be responsible.

Figure 3
Sample Project Organizer

Research Paper on Themes in *The Catcher in the Rye*

Due Dates:
Thesis statement: Tuesday, March 31
25 note cards: Thursday, April 2
Outline: Friday, April 3
First draft: Wednesday, April 8
Final draft: Wednesday, April 22

Length: Three to five (3–5) pages, not including the title page and the works cited page
Final Paper's Value: Three (3) essay grades
Overall Project Value: Four (4) homework grades, four (4) quiz grades, and three (3) essay grades

1. Possible Topics
Choose one of the following topics as the subject of your research paper:

- Attitudes of a teenager
- Teenager/parent relationships
- Dating dilemmas
- Effects of depression in a teenager's life
- Inability to accept change
- Effects of insecurity on life choices
- Profanity and the American culture
- Sibling death and how it affects living siblings
- Obsessions of young teenage men
- Behavior of an independent teenager
- High school failures
- Dormitory life for teenagers

2. Thesis Statement   *Value:* One (1) homework grade
Develop a thesis statement that defines the focus of your paper. Write the thesis on a note card and turn it in on **Tuesday, March 31.**

3. Note Cards   *Value:* Three (3) homework grades
Buy a pack of 3″ × 5″ note cards by Monday, March 30. On these note cards, write down any quotes from your research that will help to prove your thesis. (For the note card format, refer to the *Guidelines for Note Cards* handout.) You must have three (3) sources for your research paper. None of these sources may be a textbook; they must be books or articles that you have found yourself. You may use *The Catcher in the Rye* as one of your sources. You must complete and turn in at least **25 note cards** by **Thursday, April 2.**

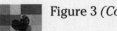

Figure 3 *(Continued)*

4. Outline   *Value:* One (1) quiz grade

Once you have conducted research and decided on the scope of your paper, outline what you will write, paragraph by paragraph. Remember: Your thesis statement will appear at the beginning of the outline. Type or neatly hand-write the one-to-two (1–2) page outline and turn it in **Friday, April 3.**

5. The Research Paper

Use your outline to write your research paper. Reminders:

• Use quotes only when they support your thoughts, not because they "sound good." Follow the class guidelines for internal documentation.

• Your thesis statement should be the last sentence in the introductory paragraph.

• Your thesis statement should be either the first or the last sentence in the concluding paragraph.

• Stay focused on your thesis statement! When the reader finishes the paper, he or she should feel convinced that you have proven your thesis to be true.

• Write, write, and write. Don't be happy with the first draft, because I won't be. Read through the paper slowly and out loud, so that you can *hear* if your paper flows smoothly.

• Write in your normal handwriting. If you have large handwriting, write five pages. If you have small handwriting, write three to four pages.

• If you are typing your paper, choose a normal font, such as Century Schoolbook, Courier, or Times New Roman in 11 or 12 points.

• Create a title page and a works cited page, following the class guidelines for references.

First Draft   *Value:* Three (3) quiz grades

Your first draft *must* include the following: ☐ a title page; ☐ an outline; ☐ a three-to-five (3–5) page research paper with internal documentation; and ☐ a works cited page. Turn in the first draft on **Wednesday, April 8.**

Final Draft   *Value:* Three (3) essay grades

Read all notes and suggestions that I have provided on your first draft, and then rewrite and retype the first draft accordingly. Your final draft must include the following: ☐ a title page; ☐ the three-to-five (3–5) page revised research paper with internal documentation; and ☐ a works cited page. Turn in the final paper on **Wednesday, April 22.**

Test Administration

*Only the flexibly creative person can really manage the future; only
the one who can face novelty with confidence and without fear.*
—Abraham Maslow

On test days, I always stretch out the rows and aisles to put more
space between the students' desks. This simple step gives the
students a visual idea of how seriously I take testing. I move those
students others might be tempted to cheat off and then balance
the seating by spreading out the rest of the class as much as
possible.

On the day before a test, I tell the students what type of test
to expect: multiple choice, short answer, essay, or a combination.
Each type of test question challenges a different level of understanding and informs the type of preparation the students will need
to undertake. I usually explain how much an essay portion of the
test will be worth, and sometimes I announce two or three possible essay topics to give students an opportunity to begin thinking
about their responses.

No matter how long you think it will take students to complete a
test, there will always be some who finish early. Prior to every test,
I remind students that when they complete their test, they are to
turn it upside down, signaling to me that they have finished. Then,
they may sit quietly with their head down, read a book, or work on
an assignment for another class. I tell them I will not bother them
until it's time to collect the test. Still, there is usually at least one
early-finisher who is wide awake, bored, and wanting to talk. I do
not disrupt the entire class with a loud "Shhh!" as this will move
the focus off the test and onto me, the meanie who is talking during that test. Instead, I get the talker a magazine, wordlessly place
it on her desk, and keep walking. I know that she'll get the message
and that, silently, she is thanking me for meeting her needs without
embarrassing her.

Questions for Reflection

1. What does the beginning of your class period look like? Is there an aspect of it that you would like to change?

2. What do you expect your students to do to show you that they are ready to begin?

3. Do you have a consistent structure throughout your lesson plan? What is it?

4. How do you organize your paperwork?

5. Is your current manner of preparing for a substitute teacher working well? How might you improve it?

6. How do you manage your textbooks' dispersal and retrieval?

7. How do you handle bathroom breaks?

8. How do you inform your students that they have homework?

9. How is test day different from any other day?

8

Expectations and Accountability

It's a funny thing about life; if you refuse to accept anything but the best, you very often get it.
—W. Somerset Maugham

I believe that students are more comfortable when they understand and agree to the limits placed on them. When students live within these limits and are able to achieve their social and academic goals in the classroom, everyone wins. When students fail to achieve these goals, everyone loses. As teachers, it's our responsibility to clarify our expectations for all aspects of our students' relationships with their classmates, their learning, and us.

Making my expectations clear shows my students that I hold them in high regard. I know that they *are* able to turn their work in on time. They *are* able to work in a group, and they *are* able to complete difficult projects successfully. Having clear expectations also shows them that I care enough to help them challenge themselves to follow the rules and to push the boundaries of understanding.

Consistently working within the same limits—whether these relate to tardiness, late work, behavior, or academics—shows my students the appropriate response to difficulty: Expectations do not change, so the individual must.

Attendance

There are two ways of spreading light; to be
The candle or the mirror that reflects it.

—Edith Wharton

At my high school, students must bring in a note from a parent within two days of an absence so that the absence can be coded "excused." I follow this rule. My students know I follow this rule, not because I tell them that I do but because I do not accept notes for absences after the second day. If they object, I simply refer them to the student handbook, handily filed on my desk, and remind them of school policy. They are not always happy, but this diffuses some of their anger toward me, and they rarely repeat the mistake.

My high school also has what is known as "code zero" absences— pre-approved, principal-authorized absences for things such as field trips, club conferences, college visits, and days when the school bus shows up late. Students occasionally try to tell me that an absence from my class was a "code zero." However, I refuse to code any absence as anything but unexcused until I receive documentation, despite protestations like "But you can ask Ms. O'Neal!" or "You know I wouldn't lie!" "Good" kid, "troublesome" kid—it does not matter. No documentation? No code zero. Students who have legitimate claims always bring the documentation by the due date.

Why all the fuss about coding an absence? Students in my high school are allowed to miss 20 school days per year. Beyond that, they automatically fail unless the district attendance committee upholds an appeal. But code zero absences do not count toward those 20 days. Honestly, I wish students only missed 20 days a year. Many of mine miss 20 days during the first semester and another 20 during the second. They are flabbergasted when their appeal is denied and they end up flunking classes because of excessive absences. The simple truth is that school is not a priority for many of my students. They sometimes miss school because they must stay home to care for younger siblings or their own children when their parents cannot get the time off from work. When a parent missing work means the family doesn't eat, there isn't a lot of debate. And when money gets tight, many of my students get jobs working 25 to 35 hours a week. Their parents are not involved in these decisions to get a job, and there are no discussions of whether the teenagers can realistically handle both work and school. When the income from a job makes the difference between riding the bus and driving a car, or between wearing hand-me-downs and wearing name-brand clothes, the student's choice is an easy one. Education suffers.

Schools have to compete with a lot that offers students more immediate fulfillment and reward. And as I've noted, there is a limit to what any individual teacher can do to make a teenage student show up in class. Still, I believe that the better we work as professionals to help our students feel the real interest and concern we have for them, and the better we nurture the love they need to have for themselves, the more likely we are to save a few of these kids from underachieving or even dropping out.

Make-Up Work

> *Every blade of grass has its Angel that bends over it and whispers,*
> *"Grow, grow."*
>
> —The Talmud

Other problems related to absenteeism are the resulting gaps in students' learning and the teacher's challenge in documenting that learning. A student at my school has five days after an absence to turn in make-up work; after that, the teacher does not have to accept it. To be honest, I did not follow this policy very closely at the beginning of my teaching career. I thought that as long as I received the work eventually, the students were documenting their learning and should receive a grade for that. I thought I was helping my students by being lenient. In fact, I was hurting them.

Here's how I came to see the light. At the end of one quarter, I found myself swamped with papers and various other assignments, most of which should have been turned in weeks earlier. I had to retrieve answer keys I'd filed away and review various lesson notes to remind myself of the assignments' specific objectives. In short, grading these papers was a real pain, and the overall quality of the student work was poor; it seemed that all this out-of-sequence work had translated into little or no learning. It was a lose–lose situation for everyone involved.

I decided to turn it into a win–win. I began by putting a big notice on my chalkboard: *Any work turned in five days after the due date will receive a zero. There are no exceptions to this rule.* I talked to my students about why I was cracking down on this policy, explaining that the work I had accepted after five days had been of poor quality and that prompt completion of missed assignments would help them in the end. After all, they wouldn't expect to understand the plot or characters in a novel—let alone *enjoy* the novel—if they read the chapters out of order and waited until after chapter 10 to read chapters 4 and 5. It was the same with the content of our course, I explained.

I left the make-up work policy statement on the board that year and have made it a part of my classroom décor ever since. Only a few students have ever attempted to exempt themselves from it. One was Derrick, a sharp kid in my advanced 11th grade English class whom I mentioned in Chapter 2. During his junior year, Derrick found the love of his life. He came from an alcoholic family where attention was a rare commodity and affection was almost nonexistent. His new relationship filled this void and easily took precedence over his schoolwork. For example, Derrick chose to walk his girlfriend all the way across campus to *her* class, even thought it meant he'd be tardy for mine. True to my policy, when he showed up late without a valid pass, I'd send him to lockout. Derrick started cutting my class with some regularity—perhaps because he resented me "pressuring" him to choose English class over precious minutes with his girlfriend. He was missing a lot of work.

I often ask my advanced juniors to work in pairs. Derrick typically teamed up with a very capable student named Ken, who I suspect would have preferred to work alone. Well, during the third quarter, the class was working in pairs on a poetry project that involved critical reading, defining terms, and creative writing. On the project organizer sheet, I stressed that each partner was responsible for turning in an individual project. Derrick and Ken appeared to be making great headway together.

On the day the poetry projects were due, Ken turned in a beautiful packet. All the work was in his handwriting—all of it, that is, except for the "and Derrick Johnson" on the title page under Ken's name. Derrick was absent, so I had to wait until the next day to tell him this was unacceptable.

When I did tell him, Derrick started to protest.

"But you said . . . ," he began, and then his voice trailed off.

"Yes, I said what?" I prompted. *(Guideline #2: Stay focused on the problem.)* No response. I told Derrick he had four more days to turn in the project. He just shook his head.

It took me two weeks to grade those poetry packets, and during that whole time I did not receive anything from Derrick. I suspect that he was waiting for me to return Ken's project so that he could copy it. When I was ready to return the packets, I asked Derrick to talk with me in the hall. *(Guideline #2: Stay focused on the problem.)*

"Derrick, you do know that it's now too late to turn in your poetry project?"

"But you said I could turn it in late," he protested.

"I said you had four days to turn it in, and that was two Fridays ago. It's been two weeks since that assignment was due."

"Can I turn it in tomorrow?"

I had to admire his tenacity, but I knew I couldn't budge on policy. "No. Now let's go back in."

Derrick flunked the third quarter with a 56 average. The day I handed out the quarter grades, I talked with him after class and asked him what he planned to do to raise his average for the remainder of the semester. *(Guideline #4: Don't sell out your values.)*

"I don't know," he replied.

"Why do you think you flunked third quarter?" I asked.

"Because you wouldn't accept my poetry project."

I pointed to the statement about late work written on the chalkboard and said, "That applies to you too."

"I know, but I thought you'd still take the project."

"Derrick, now you know what to do to raise your semester average."

"Yeah, turn work in on time."

"That's it. You can still pass for the semester, but you have to get at least a *B*– next quarter." I just laid it out there for him. *(Guideline #3: See the big picture.)* "You've earned a solid *B* in here before; you can do it again."

"Yeah," he agreed.

Work from Derrick still dribbled in late, but everything was always within the five-day window. Then came the final assignment of the year: an independent reading project that was due on the last day of class. Derrick did not turn it in. A zero on that assignment, when averaged in, would prevent him from getting the *B*– average he needed to pass my course.

I called Derrick's dad at work the day before my grades were due and explained the situation. I told Mr. Johnson I would accept his son's missing project if it was turned in by 12:30 the next day. *(Guideline #3: See the big picture.)* He thanked me and assured me that Derrick would turn it in. I added that I would leave my door unlocked so if I was at lunch or in a meeting, Derrick could place his assignment on my desk. I wanted to cover all of my bases—this kid was slippery.

The next day, I left for a faculty barbecue/meeting at noon. As we lined up to fill our plates, Derrick's French teacher approached me with a message: "Derrick asked me to tell you that he is running late because his printer is broken."

I thanked her for the message but thought, "I didn't require that the assignment be typed. It's still due at 12:30. If it's not on my desk when I get back, I won't accept it at all."

When I returned to my classroom, I saw that my desk was bare. At 2:05, Derrick walked in with his girlfriend. I looked at him, then at the clock, and then back to him. He approached my desk and held out his paper. I did not reach for it.

"Derrick," I began, "what time did your father tell you that you had to turn this paper in to me?"

"He didn't tell me a time."

A lie. Derrick had told his French teacher he was running late. How could he be running late if there wasn't a specific submission time?

I just said, "You are too late, Derrick; you just chose to flunk for the semester."

"Why did I flunk?" He still did not get it. He wanted to see his grades; he wanted me to reconsider. I told him again that he was simply too late. *(Guideline #4: Don't sell out your values.)*

It was sad, but I hoped that as he sat in a session of summer school, he realized that I was not being mean. I was holding him accountable. Some of the most important things adults teach children are to understand the way the world works, to take responsibility for their behavior, and to accept that choices have consequences. It was as if no one in Derrick's life had cared enough to make sure he understood this. I kept whispering the words that would help Derrick grow, but he was not yet ready to listen.

Sharing Your Concerns

Once you are Real you can't become unreal again.
—Margery Williams

Once I know a student will listen to me, I feel comfortable calling attention to unhealthy behavioral patterns. I will talk to him privately

about why he is not getting along with his peers or why he is flunking the class. I try to make this a friendly conference to help the student come up with real solutions.

I held one such conference with Kelvin, the student from New York whom I've mentioned. He learned to keep his boiling rage in check for me and for most of the students in our class, but there was one student who angered him easily. Her name was Shaniece. She did not come to school very often, but when she did, I could be sure she would have something negative to say about Kelvin's hair or his intelligence or the shoes he loved so much. He would get up out of his chair and lean over her, whispering threats. Shaniece would just laugh.

Kelvin and I had established a good relationship before Shaniece started this practice, so I was always able to get him back to his seat quickly and resume the lesson. However, after a few repeated incidents like this, I asked Kelvin to step outside with me.

"Hey, Kelvin, did you know that you have something on your back?" I asked.

"What?" Kelvin craned his neck to look at his back and swiped his hands up and down the back of his jacket. "C'mon, Ms. Ridnouer, what do I have on my back?"

I had his attention now. "A big red button," I said.

He eyed me warily.

"But only Shaniece and I can see it," I continued. "You let her push that button every time you let her make you mad. What can you do to hide that button?" *(Guideline #2: Stay focused on the problem.)*

"I don't know."

"Why does what she says annoy you so much?"

"She doesn't know what she's talking about," Kelvin replied angrily.

"So you're letting someone who 'doesn't know what she's talking about' control you?"

"No," he insisted, and then said, "I mean, I don't know."

"What can you do differently so *you* have control and not Shaniece?" I asked.

"I could ignore her . . . or punch her mouth until it hurts too much for her to speak." He said the last part jokingly, and I knew him well enough to know he really *was* joking.

"OK. Let's run with the first plan."

I never saw Kelvin let Shaniece push his button again. He did just what he said he would do: He ignored her. After a few times of getting no reaction, Shaniece's negative comments about Kelvin stopped completely.

Involving parents

Mary was a beautiful, otherwise-intelligent 15-year-old who allowed her friends to unduly influence her behavior. Even though she did not always *want* to do what they told her to do, she tended to do it anyway. At the beginning of the school year, Mary skipped classes often and participated infrequently when she did show up.

As I've noted, contacting parents is a standard component of my efforts to reach students who are not living up to classroom expectations. I called her mother, as did several of her other teachers. We arranged a group conference with Mary and her mom. There, we all told Mary that we wanted to get to know her, to teach her, and to see her succeed. But to do that, we needed her to come to class every day. Mary listened, and her mother was very supportive.

Mary did not skip my class again. She began sharing her ideas willingly in class, and although sometimes she did not "get" things as quickly as she would have liked, she did try, and as a result, her performance improved. Near the end of the first semester, I called her home to give her mom an update. Mary answered the phone. "Am I in trouble?" she asked.

I assured her that I was calling to tell her mom what a fantastic job she was doing in class. *(Guideline #2: Stay focused on the problem.)*

"Really?" Mary asked. "Please call back tomorrow. My mom's not here right now. She needs to hear something good about me. My math teacher called yesterday with a bad report."

I promised I would, and when I did speak with Mary's mother the following day, the warmth I heard in her voice told me that she was beaming with pride. Parents of struggling teenagers are so used to getting phone calls about their children's negative behavior that a phone call about positive behavior can have a huge impact. Mary became even more of an asset after that. She modeled good behavior and problem-solving techniques. She stepped up to instruct other students who were confused or displayed poor behavior. She really helped build camaraderie in the class.

I can tell a similar story about Jermaine, a wholly different kind of student. Jermaine's IQ was below average and he was usually withdrawn and defensive. At first, he took all of my efforts to help him understand a concept as affirmation that he was less capable than others in the class. However, over time, he began to trust me, and some new behaviors began to emerge. *(Guideline #3: See the big picture.)*

Jermaine no longer engaged in conversation with one of his more argumentative classmates. He began taking notes and speaking up when he was confused. I noticed but didn't say anything. I believe that if I'd commented on Jermaine's new behaviors, he would have become very self-conscious about them, and I worried that he might revert to his old ways "to get me back" if he ever perceived that I had "done him wrong." So I kept quiet, he continued these behaviors, and his grade rose from an *F* to a *D* to a *C.* After a few months of watching Jermaine make steady progress, I called his home. I told his mother about my initial troubles with him, but then I explained how he and I had worked together to overcome them. She was thrilled.

This is just a snapshot of the kind of good that can come from sticking by students and calling parents when the students decide to believe in themselves and tend to their responsibilities. Each phone call takes only five minutes, but the effects are a positive ripple in the negative pool of thoughts common to struggling students and their parents.

Calling students

If I'm concerned about a student, and I do not feel that I am reaching him or her through one-on-one talks at school, I sometimes call that

student at home. I call the *student,* not a parent. I have called about missing assignments, disappointing behavior, and just general concern. One phone call that I made was to Kim. She had transferred into my advanced English 11 class well into the third quarter, and by that time we were functioning more like a group of peers discussing literary ideas than a teacher leading students through a curriculum. Kim, frankly, did not fit in. She griped, complained, and attempted to manipulate me. She was also absent a lot and fell behind with her work.

At first, I met Kim's complaints with nonverbal warnings: a sharp look, steady eye contact, and a head shake. *(Guideline #1: Don't let students fast-talk you.)* And I continued doing this for longer than I might usually because so many of her classmates chose to simply ignore her. They did not want her to rock the boat we had been sailing so smoothly. I thought Kim would catch a clue from them. She didn't. She grew worse.

We started reading *Song of Solomon* by Toni Morrison, and Kim hated it. Then she attempted to bully me into allowing a class vote about whether we should continue reading the book or not. Although her attempt was not successful, I'd had enough. I called her at home that night. I told Kim that I suspected that she was a bright young woman, but she had not given me any concrete evidence to support this intuition of mine. I suggested to her that she register for regular English 12 for the next school year because the advanced course did not seem to suit her pacing and academic needs. *(Guideline #4: Don't sell out your values.)*

Kim was quiet on the other end of the line. I went on to tell her that for the upcoming independent reading assignment, she would need to choose a novel that had *not* been made into a movie.

She stopped being quiet. "But why?" she whined. "That's not fair! I am already halfway done with a novel."

I explained. "I overheard you bragging to Melissa that you didn't really read your last independent reading selection, that you had simply watched the movie. I didn't give you a zero then because I had already turned in my grades. But for this upcoming selection, I want to make sure that you *read* and don't just watch a movie adaptation."

"I read half of the other novel," Kim said.

"But you received a grade for the *entire* novel," I replied. "You didn't earn that grade, yet you still received it. That is hardly fair." *(Guideline #2: Stay focused on the problem.)*

I ended the conversation telling Kim that I expected her to get on board with the rest of the class by stopping the complaining and the constant absenteeism.

Well, she stopped the complaining and accepted her assignments when she was in class, but Kim never did become a fully participating student. The attendance committee denied her attendance appeal for my class and for each of her other classes, and she had to repeat every class she took during her first semester at our school. She thought that if she simply insisted on getting her way, she would get it. She had to learn the hard way that the system does not work to fit the individual; the individual has to work to fit the system. On the bright side, she did model for my other students the kind of behavior that would cause a person to flunk.

My goal in calling Kim at home was to get her involved in my class and to help her succeed there. Although the phone call fell short of this goal, it did allow me to keep the rest of the class on course. My hope is that Kim will remember that phone call when she is trying to figure out what she needs to do to pass future classes.

Happily, I can point to many student phone calls that had clearly successful outcomes. When I called Reginald, Chelsea, and Brian about their missing assignments, they took that time on the phone to ask questions they had been uncomfortable asking in class. Each one of them took the phone call as the wake-up call that I meant it to be. Each one of them passed easily.

This personal touch only takes a few minutes, and it really can make a difference. It does not necessarily change the behavior you want to change, and it might not even change the *student* you want to change, but it will still cause a change in other ways. Word will get around that you call home, and this alone is enough to keep many students in the "in" zone. The last thing these kids want is to have their teacher calling home for *any* reason. You may also find, as I

have, that awareness of this policy will prompt other students to "slip up" so they can get some attention from you. Give it to them. They are worth your time.

When a Student Chooses to Fail

We are most deeply asleep at the switch when we fancy we control any switches at all.

—Annie Dillard

I always struggle with myself about the kid who chooses to fail no matter what I do. These are the kids who don't see any reason to pass and can't see a reason for attending school beyond the fact that showing up seems to make everyone stop yelling at them. Sure, at report card time they have to brace themselves for their parents' lectures, threats, and anger, but report cards only come out four times a year.

Demontre, a junior, was a typical case. He would get into fights and be suspended. He would transfer out of our school and then transfer back in. He would encourage his mother to second-guess his teachers and blame them for his failure. He would arrive late or repeatedly sleep in class, ignore my warnings, and then wonder why I sent him to lockout. He would accuse me of wanting him to be uneducated.

I called Demontre's mother multiple times. We spoke in the evenings when she had returned home from work, but she was tired after her long day and did not seem to really want to hear about this son of hers. So she would yell at me about my tone of voice. A few times, she called me a racist. It was only after many phone calls that we were finally able to move our conversation beyond these non-issues and get to the real problem: Demontre was doing nothing in class. Demontre's mom wanted me to write down all his missing assignments and give him ample time to complete them. I explained that keeping track of assignments was the student's responsibility. Then

I explained the homework board and the five-day limit on sub-mitting late work. She asked me if I would please make this one exception. I agreed. Demontre was still something of a mystery to me. Had I been confident that he was capable of the work and just refusing to do it, I would not have made this exception to my five-day policy. I hoped that this one last chance would be the chance we both needed: his chance to show me what he was really made of and mine to begin to forge a connection with this disconnected kid. *(Guideline #3: See the big picture.)*

I sat down and wrote out each of Demontre's missed assign-ments, providing extensive directions and reference to the materials and readings he would need. I gave this assignment packet to him the next time I saw him in class, which was about a week later. Two weeks after that, he finally turned in an assignment . . . but it was one that I had not given. When I immediately gave it back to him, Demon-tre got mad, called me a liar, and stormed out of the room.

I talked to his mother that evening. Here it was, the end of sec-ond quarter, and the only assignment Demontre had turned in was one I had not assigned. Demontre's mom asked me if her son was passing. I wanted to scream. Instead, I calmly explained the situation and told her I would accept any work Demontre had to give me up until the end of second quarter. After that, it would be too late. He would receive an *F.*

She agreed, but days passed and I still received nothing from Demontre. His mother and I continued to talk once a week for the next month. I felt as though I was wasting my time. I told her that I would like her to be the one to call me with concerns because I had already shared all of mine. I gave her my home phone number. She never called.

I saw Demontre sporadically for the rest of the year, but he never lasted an entire class period in my room. He never assimilated to my expectations. I think I have figured out the reasoning behind his behavior: Demontre's mom was the only parent he had, and she was full of false threats. Still, he knew time was running out before even his mother would become sick of his irresponsible behavior and

insist that he get a fulltime job—a job, Demontre concluded, that would be hard, miserable, and poorly paid, and that he would have to do for the rest of his life. So he was using his time in high school to relax. The only future he could conceive of was so depressing and unappealing that he couldn't begin to think about choosing another path. He had resigned himself to this, and there was nothing I could do about it.

Darrin was another student similar to Demontre but with three important differences: He was younger, he took responsibility for his actions, and he didn't have any behavior problems. At the beginning of the year, Darrin was passing freshman English with a *D*. By the middle of the year his work output had trickled down to almost nothing, and he was flunking with an average in the teens. Again, I followed the usual steps, but there was no change in his performance. I talked to him and to his mom regularly, but nothing I said or did could make Darrin do the work.

At the end of the year, Darrin explained it all to me in just a few lines in his closing letter: "What I liked this year is how I came in and tried for a little bit. But now that I'm not trying, I'm not learning and I hate myself instead of hating this class." He accepted responsibility for his failure. I was not thrilled to hear him say he hated himself, but at least he was not scapegoating, as Demontre was. Because of this, I'm hopeful about Darrin's chance of succeeding as he continues on in school.

Encouraging Exploration

When you perform . . . you are out of yourself—larger and more potent, more beautiful. You are for minutes heroic. This is power. This is glory on earth. And it is yours, nightly.

—Agnes de Mille

Students are conditioned to expect two things: to be told what to think and to be told what to do. Instead of giving them what they expect, I try to surprise them by taking a constructivist approach in my

instruction. Instead of telling them what to think, I prod them to explore a subject themselves. I do the same with discipline by encouraging them to explore the reasoning behind our class rules. Academically and behaviorally, the students construct their own understanding that correlates to their personal experiences and interests. This understanding proves to be a much more effective guiding force than any explanations I could give.

Obviously, it is easier to simply tell students what to study and what to remember than it is to encourage them to explore a subject. But teachers who choose the easier way do so despite knowing intuitively or through experience that true learning is that which engages the mind and causes a person to wonder and wander in search of answers.

Through my questioning style, I encourage reflection in my students. Sometimes I pique their interest by asking questions in Spanish or in my approximation of their regional dialect. Those who can translate what I have asked repeat the questions in English (or standard English) for themselves and their classmates and feel that much smarter for being able to do so. It's a good attention getter when a discussion is on the wane.

Unorthodox Engagement

> *The teacher who is attempting to teach without inspiring the pupil with a desire to learn is hammering on a cold iron.*
> —Horace Mann

I know that people will perform at a higher, more creative level if they are led to believe that this higher level is attractive and possible. Standards-based curricula are good starting points for introducing a new concept, but they can't possibly be a good fit for all students. My lower-income, minority students often read one or more grade levels below their actual grade, and their reading comprehension lags even further. In order to improve both decoding skills and comprehension, I supplement the set curriculum with high-interest literature that appeals to my students' maturity level, areas of interest, and racial identity. In reaching out to these students and caring about them, I come to know them as people with feelings of shame, a good sense of their deficiencies, *and* healthy esteem for what they can do and what they have accomplished. All these factors influence my instructional decisions. The challenge for all teachers is to figure out what kind of lessons will appeal to and enhance the achievement of their specific group of kids.

My students love it when we chant answers to grammar questions, and they listen attentively when their classmates give speeches. Some of my colleagues think I am nuts for straying from the suggested reading list and incorporating public speaking and card playing into my lesson plan. My defense is that I must engage my students and these approaches are what works. They crack open the door to learning; once that door is cracked, I can push it wide open.

Keeping Expectations High

Whatever you can do or dream you can, begin it;
Boldness has genius, power and magic in it.
—Johann Wolfgang von Goethe

At the end of the school year, many teachers resign themselves to the fact that the students are not going to do the work, and so they don't bother assigning much. I hold another view. At this point in the year, I have had these students for three and one-half quarters; they are ready for my most challenging assignments yet. They understand my teaching style and have matured since the beginning of the year. This is not the time to give up on them! It's time to impress upon them all that they really can do.

Here is what I did one year. My district requires all 12th graders to complete a senior exit project, which involves an oral presentation. I wanted to give my 11th graders the opportunity to learn and practice this skill, but I didn't want to leave out my 9th graders. It's never too early to learn how to present yourself in public. I designed the three following lessons and received many interesting comments about each.

Freshman English

My 9th graders had just finished reading *Animal Farm*. Instead of assigning a five-paragraph essay on the themes found in the novel, I wanted to give them a chance to employ some of the tactics that the animals in the novel use to gain power. The answer: an assignment to work through the democratic process and elect a representative. To include the element of public speaking, one step of the project involved each student writing and giving a speech about why he or she should be elected as class representative.

I modeled a speech for the class, and together we discussed the written elements and the presentation elements of my speech. Then they plunged into writing their own speeches on a controversial issue but soon stalled. They were not comfortable with choosing a side to the issue.

"Which side is correct?" they asked me.

"Either side is correct, as long as you can defend it," I replied.

They were boggled. We brainstormed some reasons in support of both sides, and then they plunged back into the writing.

On speech day, I noticed that my freshmen had combed their hair a little more neatly. Their clothes were a little nicer. They were nervous but trying to act cool about it. One by one, they rose, gave their speeches, and knocked my socks off. They were convincing; I would certainly vote for them. I received more effort from some of the students for this assignment than I had received all year. They had connected with the assignment, and even though their speeches brought about no "real" change, they understood the lesson and were pleased with their performance.

When they were giving their speeches, they looked as cool as cucumbers. When I read their closing letters, I found out they had actually felt differently. Queena told me, "The most memorable assignment was us doing our speeches cause people were nervous but they did it anyway." They also expanded what they thought was possible for them to do. Helena wrote this:

> What I love most about English class is writing. After this year, my passion for writing got more specific. Now I love to write persuasive essays. As you can see my writing has probably improved but my spelling has not. The most memorable assignment this year was when we gave our speeches. We had to persuade others to see things from our perspective.

What connections she had made. This assignment pushed Helena's writing skills to a new level. She could have never accomplished this through a five-paragraph essay assignment. The energy of interclass connections bred creativity and achievement.

Junior English

Students in my regular English 11 class read *A Raisin in the Sun* and wanted to act it out. We chose the props we needed and who would bring them in. Then I assigned roles. For everyone to have a speaking part, each character would have to be played by a different student in each scene.

We talked about the dramatic skills needed, and a few students even acted them out in front of the class to provide a concrete example—modeling at its best!

Each scene's cast practiced reading and performing their material, and then we put on the play. Not only did *I* critique each student's performance, but so did each student. They had to offer one piece of positive and one piece of negative (if applicable) feedback for each student performing. I had the arduous task of cutting and collating the comments for each student, but it was worth it. They were quiet as church mice when I gave them their stack of comments back. The written word proved its power that day.

Advanced junior English

My advanced 11th graders had finished reading *Song of Solomon*. To help them understand the theme of identity that runs throughout the book, I assigned each student a different poem or short story dealing with identity. They then had to write a one- to three-minute speech summarizing their selection and comparing it with *Song of Solomon*. Finally, I asked them to write a four-paragraph essay with documentation fully explaining two ways in which the two pieces were related. The form of this project was very similar to the senior exit project they would be completing during the next school year.

They complained, but they soon started working when they saw the due dates listed in the project organizer: speeches were only two days away! Well, those students gave some of the most convincing speeches I have ever heard. They maintained good eye contact and posture. The best part was the pride I saw in them. When they received the feedback from the other students and me, they just beamed.

If there is one thing I have found it is that if a kid believes he cannot do something, he is right. My students were nervous speaking in public, but it was my expectation that they could do it. This expectation served as the boost they needed to prove to themselves that they could speak in public. I closed the school year confident that the next time a teacher gave my students a speaking assignment, they would have no doubt in their abilities, and they would be able to concentrate even more on the quality of their ideas.

In Praise of Praise (and a Little Candy)

> *Happiness is not a destination. It is the attitude with which you choose to travel.*
>
> —Yogi Arit Desal

Don't you love it when someone pats you on the back and tells you that you've done a good job? Students love it too.

When a discussion or activity goes especially well, I make a point to thank the students at the end of class. It's something I do sparingly and only on those magical days. Kids know when praise is real, and when they get it, they just glow.

Although we don't want to shower our students with fake praise, we don't want to chastise too freely either. On those "we're-just-cooperating-because-we-have-to-be-here" days, when the kids are sluggish and not involved, it can be tempting to gripe. ("You guys are just draining the life out of me. Wake up!") I try to remember that if *I* am not doing anything to engage my students, I shouldn't be putting them down for not being engaged.

Sometimes a teacher can just feel when a class needs a little boost. You see it in their eyes: They are tired, hungry, or bored. On these occasions, I will look at my students and say, "Man, you guys look wiped out. Will a little sugar help?" This question alone puts a spark in their eyes. I proceed to pass out one Starburst to each kid and then move on with the day. With a little square of candy, they move right along with me.

I also use the candy to say thank you when I catch everyone in the class doing a good job. Sometimes during a writing assignment I will look up and see everyone working. Pens and pencils are flashing across white paper, and I can almost see the ideas flying. As they finish up, I silently walk around the room placing a piece of candy on the corner of each student's desk. Most of them whisper a thank you or at least smile. Some even show their appreciation by continuing to write and eating the candy later.

I generally use the candy in the first semester only. By second semester, my kids are in the groove, behaving and reacting in class according to our class rules because they want to. They do not need an external reward because they have an internal one—pride.

Questions for Reflection

1. What are your rules regarding late work from students?

2. How does the relationship you have with a student help you address that student's academic or social problems?

3. Describe a classroom problem or concern that would warrant a phone call to a student's parent.

4. Under what circumstances would you call a student at home?

5. How do you manage a student who is choosing to fail?

6. What might you do to cultivate wonder in your classroom?

7. How do you keep your expectations high throughout the school year?

8. What are some of the ways you praise students for a job particularly well done?

9

The Students, the Curriculum, and You

And the day came when the risk to remain tight in the bud was more painful than the risk it took to blossom.

—Anaïs Nin

Teaching is a creative act. It's the attempt to help students create something in their minds that was not there before. St. Francis of Assisi explains that a person who works with his hands is a laborer; a person who works with his hands and his head is a craftsperson; and a person who works with his hands, his head, and his heart is an artist. The question is, which of these would you like to be—a laborer, a craftsperson, or an artist?

A teacher who delivers monotone lectures from behind a podium is a laborer. One whose lectures include voice modulation and questions for the students is a craftsperson. But a teacher who comes out from behind the podium, asks questions, interjects personal stories, offers a variety of visual examples, and speaks in different voices is an artist. The artist is the kind of teacher students connect with the most.

Teachers can often plan and organize the "hands" and "head" parts of a lesson prior to class time. The "heart" parts, though, tend to be impromptu. For example, you generally don't plan to dance a jig or perform birdcalls to get students' attention or pull them into the lesson. You just do it.

But just as there are all kinds of artists and artistic styles, there are all kinds of teachers and teaching styles. Think of all the teachers who taught you. What did they do to gain your attention, to really get you to learn? Maybe dancing and birdcalls are a bit kooky for you. Perhaps you are not one to put on character voices as you read aloud to students or to act out the cat-footed approach of Carl Sandburg's "Fog." But you might invite students to do these things for you. And if singing a folk song in front of the class gives you hives, consider having the entire class sing along with you. Be the artist that *you* are and no other. It's up to all of us to find our particular classroom persona: our way of gaining students' attention and really focusing that attention on learning.

Rekindling a Love of Learning

The conflict between what one is and who one is expected to be touches all of us. And sometimes, rather than reach for what one could be, we choose the comfort of the failed role, preferring to be the victim of circumstance, the person who didn't have a chance.

—Merle Shain

All teachers want to help their students love the act and process of learning, but we know how challenging this can be. By the time many students arrive in your classroom, their sense of curiosity has been thoroughly stomped on. Past teachers and their parents have told them that there is just one right answer. They aren't used to having the freedom to explore the myriad ways of attacking every problem.

I think this is why writing seems like such an impossible task to so many of my high school students: They have a difficult time understanding that there is not one right way to write an essay. I tell them to start the way that best suits them, and I focus on giving them the tools to find out what *their* way is. We talk about webbing, outlining, free writing, and many other writing starters. In the beginning, they ask, "Yeah, but which one is the 'right' one?"

I stick to my guns and say, "The right way is the way that generates the best ideas for *you.* Pick one that appeals to you and try it out." After they see that I grade each type of prewriting exercise on the quality of its ideas, they begin to trust me and use the method they are the most comfortable with for future writing assignments. And as the year goes on, more and more of them come to understand that what I want from them is to logically explain and support their ideas. What emerges is truly inspiring. Consider this, from Ken:

> I was thinking about what Emerson said about pathways in our brain and how it's easier to stay in preset paths than it is to create new pathways. I think Milkman [the main character in Toni Morrison's *Song of Solomon*] is learning this lesson. He's finally questioning what his parents have taught him.

This is why I love teaching. Not only had Ken integrated Emerson's ideas into *his* life, he had come to see them in a literary character's life too. It's a perfect example of the level of thinking, learning, and understanding we want all our students to experience. When we give students the tools of analysis and how to seek out relevance to their lives, they can learn anything.

Something as simple as a line in a play can provide the spark that a student needs to find meaning and purpose in the curriculum. In Lorraine Hansberry's *A Raisin in the Sun,* Mama says this to Beneatha:

> Child, when do you think is the time to love somebody the most; when they done good and made things easy for everybody? Well then, you ain't through learning—because that ain't the time at all. It's when he's at his lowest and can't believe in hisself 'cause the world done whipped him so.

This really struck me as the truth. I had watched the movie and read that play many times, but I did not connect with this speech until I was with one particular class. After these lines, I stopped the reading and we talked about them. I asked the students where they could see examples of this in their own lives. Because they were hesitant to speak up, I shared how it is easy to love my husband when he is in a good mood. However, when his mood is sour or when he is preoccupied or angry with someone at work, it is a little tougher for me to love him. Still, that is when he needs me most, so I do not abandon him; I help him through in whatever way I can.

At this point, one student and then another and another began opening up, sharing information about their relationships with girlfriends, boyfriends, and parents. One boy, Brian, was positively struck and kept saying, "Yeah, I know what you mean." I could almost hear the synapses firing in his brain.

One week later, this same young man was walking his girlfriend, Robin, to my class. (They had class with me at different times.) She seemed to be upset about something. I said hello, and she managed a smile back. Brian looked as though he was taking her state of mind personally.

"Brian, I've had a bad day," Robin snapped. "Leave me alone." She had almost reached her breaking point.

Brain said, "Fine. Forget you," half joking, half serious.

Because I knew them both well, I was comfortable saying to him, "Remember what Mama said? How it was hard to love someone who is down, but it's when that person needs you the most?" *(Guideline #4: Don't sell out your values.)*

He smiled and said, "Oh, yeah." Then he looked at his girlfriend softly. "Robin, I'll see you later," he said. She waved goodbye to him and smiled a thank you to me.

I also like Mama's speech to Beneatha because it summarizes my basic philosophy about kids. It's easy to love the ones who are manageable and motivated; it's more difficult to love the ones who are apathetic and annoying. But it's these latter kids who need us most. If we keep showing them that we will be there with them *no matter what,* they will eventually believe us and trust us enough to help them build self-confidence as learners and people.

A child must feel that someone loves him unconditionally in order to have the confidence that he is lovable and that he can trust his decisions and do well. Success becomes possible. It is irresponsible for educators to assume that this type of person is already in a child's life before that child enters our classroom. Many of the kids we teach do not come from nurturing homes. Many attend or have previously attended overcrowded schools where teachers and administrators are frustrated by the difficulty they have fulfilling their educational mission.

As teachers, we have the choice to be one of the overworked who teaches a subject or to be one of the overworked who teaches *students*. My point is that we're going to be overworked either way, so why not chose the option that can energize us? When we place *students* before subjects, we have fewer discipline problems, more smiles, fewer parent conferences, and more compliments. These are reason enough to make the choice.

Life Lessons

Your work is to discover your work and then with all your heart to give yourself to it.

—Buddha

Most adolescents are under the impression that teachers simply do not understand a student's plight in life: the daily difficulties that arise from dealing with parents, siblings, seven different teachers, coaches, and administrators. I try to show my students that this isn't so. I tell them about my own experience with these situations in hopes of opening a forum for them to discuss the people in their lives that drive them nuts. Then we "problem solve" in writing. I make sure to join them.

We all share our writing when we finish. I impress upon them the truth that as adults, they will come in contact with difficult and incompetent people every day. I explain how I deal with these challenges. I talk about my husband's difficulties doing the same. This helps the student move away from the "I'm the only one in this situation" attitude to "I need to learn how to get a handle on this now. These people aren't going away."

It's common for people in general and adolescents in particular to feel as though they are alone in dealing with a problem. The more we can work to reduce this isolated feeling, the more we improve the mental heath of our student population and the future generation of leaders.

Teach to What Students Know

No man can reveal to you aught but that which already lies half asleep in the dawning of your knowledge.
—Kahlil Gibran

Every teacher's challenge is to provide each student a path from what he already knows to new insight and knowledge. This sometimes involves reviewing subject-relevant terms or rules. It sometimes involves persuading students that they are capable of completing challenging tasks and mastering complex content. It's up to us to tap into the desire to make sense of the world that each child is born with but may have allowed to go to sleep.

I realized the truth of this for myself while I was a student in a seminar and internship offered through South Dakota State University. My fellow interns and I were inundated with information about the Lakota people with whom we would soon be working. One symbol they taught us was the medicine wheel, and its basic concept is that every person has four essential parts: mental, spiritual, physical, and emotional. Each part is represented as a line within a wheel, and each line needs to be the same length if the wheel is to turn smoothly. I connected strongly and immediately with this symbol because it expressed clearly an idea about the need for personal balance that I'd always felt intuitively. The medicine wheel tapped into a concept that I had previously been unable to visualize or verbalize.

This inability to express the balance that I needed in my life was the very reason I was in South Dakota that summer: I was on a quest! The medicine wheel became the "in" for me to invest in learning about and working with the Lakota people.

Our students need an "in" to each of their subjects, and we must work to discover the possible points of entry. A good place to start is with things that evoke emotional response. Slavery is a subject that fits the bill for my students. Even though more than 80 percent of my students are black, very few of them know anything specific about slavery. Our unit on slave literature gives them the opportunity to connect with the subject—something that they might be too angry, ashamed, or afraid to research on their own. We read Harriet Jacobs's true account of her life in slavery. We read poetry by "Uncle Tom" slaves and essays by white people who believed slavery was justified. I give extra credit to those who visit a museum or see a movie focused on slaves. I know my students have connected with the material when they start talking about previous generations of their families who had been slaves. There is pride in their voices where once there might have been shame.

Here I am, a white woman whose family is from the Midwest and most likely did not participate in the Civil War. Who am I to teach them about slavery? They choose to learn with me because they see a bridge from themselves to the material in the class. They see the curriculum's implications in their reality.

The Value of Education

Knowledge of what you love somehow comes to you; you don't have to read nor analyze nor study. If you love a thing enough, knowledge of it seeps into you, with particulars more real than any chart can furnish.

—Jessamyn West

Why do you teach the subject you teach? If you're like me, you teach it because it intrigues you. You love to think about it. You can remember weird facts about it when you cannot remember other trivia, such as how long a senator is in office or the current price for chicken breasts. You teach your subject because you love it. But like other loves, if it is neglected, the passion fizzles. We owe it to our students to stay intrigued with our subject and to be the lifelong learner we tell our students to be. This is the way to plan lessons that will spark magic responses from students who would much rather be watching an MTV reality show.

As teachers, we have to set up situations that give the students choices that they never thought possible. Sunny Decker, the author of *An Empty Spoon,* was right when she said, "They've got to discover their own truth, if it's to be a part of them." Michael exemplified this in his closing letter, in which I ask students to tell me their most memorable assignment: "My most memorable assignment was when we had to read three pages of *Animal Farm* for homework. I ended up reading the whole book that night. I think sometimes I get a little carried away in my readings."

There is a pride in these words that cannot be given *to* someone *by* someone else. It's a gift one gives oneself. Michael chose to give himself the gift of finishing a book on his own volition. Now he knows that choice is available to him, and the odds are higher that he will make that choice again with another book. In the end, he stretched his view of himself just a little bit.

Students get in the habit of dismissing certain choices that their teachers give them. They will say, "That's too hard!" or "I can't do that" or "My mom always said I stunk at math." *(Guideline #1: Don't let students fast-talk you.)* Each of these statements sends the same message: "That assignment is not a choice for me." I hear this message loud and clear when I introduce my poetry unit to my 11th graders. Many of them balk at the possibility they could understand or write poetry. I listen and explain my expectations. *(Guideline #2: Stay focused on the problem.)* I tell them poetry is one of my favorite types of writing because it is so concise, so concentrated. We talk about how someone calling you a derogatory name makes your body react. Your heart races; your temples throb. "That's what poetry is," I tell them. "It's powerful stuff in only a few words." Around me, heads begin to nod. It's a deep concept, but they understand because they can relate to the situation I use as my example.

It's at this point in the lesson that I have to do something dramatic—something to really hook them before I lose them. I choose to expose my heart and my life to my kids by bringing in my own writing and reading a journal entry and the poem that came from that entry. *(Guideline #4: Don't sell out your values.)* The students study their copies of my work. They are intrigued. They may still see understanding and writing poetry as a mountain to climb, but it's likely they can finally understand why the effort might be worthwhile. At this point, my job becomes giving them the tools that will serve as their climbing gear and starting them off at the base of the mountain. We review a list of literary terms, define them, and then look for examples of them in my poem. Someone identifies imagery. Someone else mentions metaphor. But those are the only techniques listed that we see.

"Oh, so all of these literary techniques aren't used in each poem?" someone innocently asks. It's the kind of question a lot of high school students have but don't want to ask for fear of exposing ignorance of something they "should already know." But because the student feels comfortable in the class, he feels comfortable asking the question. It gives us a great segue into a discussion of why writers use literary techniques. *(Guideline #2: Stay focused on the problem.)*

Ultimately, my students read poetry that they end up saying is too easy (!), and they read poetry they say is hard but not impossible. They write their own poetry and participate in a poetry slam, where everyone reads at least one original poem and whoever gets the most applause moves on to the next round. The students eagerly support one another with their comments: "Man, that's deep," and "You go, girl!" They feed off each other's energy. And quiet students regularly surprise everyone with really beautiful work. I think particularly of Sean, a shy kid whose poem about God and death just floored us all.

The poetry unit concludes with an exam that asks students to analyze poetry they have never read before. If I'd told them at the beginning of the unit that they would have to do this, they would have crumpled. Now, though, they are ready for a challenge. Give them a poem, any poem, and they can figure it out.

To prepare for this rigorous exam, we play a review game where students work in teams to analyze poetry they have never seen before. Competition is fierce, and I watch with pride as my students astutely analyze Dickinson and Shakespeare along with Angelou and Hughes.

Some of the closing letters to me mention this poetry unit. Dave was a big kid who expressed himself slowly when he spoke but eagerly in his writing. He wrote, "The most memorable assignment this year was when we had to write poems, because that is nothing but feeling." He came to know that because feelings are a part of him, poetry could be a part of him too. His eyes were opened to new choices.

T. J. informed me that poetry was now in his range of choices as well. He wrote, "When we were able to write poems, it showed me that writing poems really has to come from the heart. From reading these poems, I somehow developed a liking to poetry." I should mention that T. J. was an attractive football player who came from a home with its share of problems. He connected with literature in a way he never thought possible. His worldview expanded. I knew I'd succeeded.

How to Tap into Students' Interests

Nothing in the world can take the place of Persistence. Talent will not; nothing is more commonplace than unsuccessful men with talent. Genius will not; unrewarded genius is almost a proverb. Education alone will not; the world is full of educated derelicts. Persistence and Determination alone are omnipotent.

—Calvin Coolidge

I am always listening to what my students say to get hints about their interests. This tells me what I can incorporate into the classroom that they will respond to without a hard sell. For example, rap is not a musical genre that I am particularly fond of, but I try to stay aware of the latest rap artists.

At the end of class one day a few years ago, I heard Lamar and Kelvin talking about the raps they had written. I meandered over and asked if I could read one. They obliged, and I made the observation that many rappers look and act dumb but are actually really smart people. Kelvin gave me a wary eye.

I continued: "I saw Coolio on television with his normal Buckwheat hairdo. He was on a talk show, and I didn't think he'd have anything intelligent to contribute. I was wrong. He was articulate, logical, and downright persuasive."

Kelvin chimed in with, "Yeah, rappers look like that because it sells. Clean-cut doesn't sell."

Then the bell rang, ending our potentially interesting discussion of why clean-cut does not sell, but I was pleased to have been able to connect with two boys about a subject that was meaningful to them. I picked up on a new sense of appreciation from the two of them after that. It's almost as if they could tolerate my interests and me better because I tolerated them and theirs, and this brought us one step closer to acceptance and understanding.

Use your own insight into student interests to inform your classroom decisions. Follow up on your impression that the class clown is really bright but has no outlet for his intelligence. Find out what interests him by watching to see when his eyes light up. Ask him to teach a lesson on a topic he loves. Trust that he'll be about to present content in a manner that will resonate with his peers, and consider that he might identify a means of connecting to content that never would have occurred to you.

Creating "Relatable" Assignments

It is your work in life that is the ultimate seduction.
—Pablo Picasso

The more the students connect with the assignments, the better their work will be. I find this to be true when, after reading a novel, each class and I brainstorm that novel's themes, and these themes become possible topics for a research paper. (See the Sample Project Organizer on page 130.) I choose each novel deliberately from the list of possibilities provided in my curriculum. If my students are grappling with issues surrounding friendship, we read *A Separate Peace,* where a boy's jealousy of his friend leads to tragedy. If they are struggling to use appropriate language in the classroom, we read *The Catcher in the Rye;* they get the chance to curse when we read out loud, which leads to conversations about word choice as the means to effective communication. If they are struggling with all the rules in their life, we read *Animal Farm,* and they experience how rules can shape and misshape a group. When it's time for them to work on research papers, they will already have an emotional connection to the topic they choose along with opinions that will serve to support their thesis statement and guide their research.

After students select a topic and submit it to me, I go to the public library and pull various titles that relate to the selected themes. This shows my personal investment in their work, gives them a jump start on their research, and augments our school library's limited resources. And during our three days of in-class research, my students work hard to find out information on "their" theme. They write about teen dating, depression, alcohol abuse, and sexually transmitted diseases. I hear students say, "I didn't know there were books out there like this."

In her closing letter, Cynthia wrote this:

> My most memorable assignment was the research paper on *The Catcher in the Rye.* I didn't hate the assignment. I actually really did enjoy it because it was so easy. I mean sure we had to do a lot of research and follow a lot of steps, but it was my first real research paper.

Research is easy? Following steps is enjoyable? When you take the time to relate your lesson to students' interests, you'll find that they become naturally engaged in even the most challenging assignment.

It's a win for everyone. Julia, a foreign exchange student from Brazil, wrote this:

> The most memorable assignment was when we read *The Catcher in the Rye,* and I wrote about teenagers seeking freedom and their responsibilities. That is what is happening to me now. I'm living in another country, I have many responsibilities, and if I get in trouble, I'm by myself and I have to solve it. So the research I did for that assignment helped me in life too.

I love the pride that resonates in this comment. And not only was Julia able to relate to the novel and develop a theme into a thesis statement and a five-page research paper, but she actually found information that helped her evaluate her life. I could not have asked for more!

Flexibility with Lesson Plans

Flops are part of life's menu and I'm never a girl to miss out on a course.

—Rosalind Russell

Sometimes students respond more positively to a lesson plan t han we could have hoped; other times, they reject it entirely. The challenge is to take both scenarios in stride. Analyze each lesson plan for its strengths and its weaknesses, but keep in mind that every group of students has its own chemistry. The activity that soared during second period could easily flop in third period.

This happened to me when I was teaching my 9th graders about satire and we read Mark Twain's "Encounter with an Interviewer." The second period kids loved it; they handled the follow-up questions with ease and wanted to read the story again. Because of their enthusiasm, I decided to jump into the next day's lesson: writing a satire of their own. The students were excited and even wanted to act their satires out in front of their classmates.

After this, I was understandably pumped up about this lesson. I couldn't wait to see how my third period students would react. Well, they didn't react at all. They thought Mark Twain was dumb and that satire was even dumber. They didn't find the story the least bit funny. What could I say? Trying to explain why something is funny is like explaining how to knit by unraveling a sweater: Soon you end up with a bunch of nothing.

The students and I trudged through the questions just so I could make sure that they had paid attention during the reading. They answered all of the questions correctly, but without any hint of enthusiasm. I saw that the rest of that day's lesson would be a bust and that tomorrow's—actually writing a satire—would flop too. It was time for me to think on my feet and make up new lesson plans right then.

We moved to a more concrete piece by Annie Dillard about nighttime and monsters. The third period students perked up. *This* they could relate to. They told me that it reminded them of times from their own childhood, and just like that, I had the inspiration I needed for a new writing assignment: *Tell your childhood monsters-at-night story in the same fashion that Annie Dillard tells hers.*

Everyone came out learning something. They did not learn exactly what I had set out to teach them, but I was still able to address my greater objective: helping students understand a new writing style and its associated techniques, including establishing a setting, building suspense, and creating a satisfying ending. I had to be flexible enough to allow this kind of mid-lesson change, or I would've lost not only the attention of my students but also their trust. My students rely on me to "read" them; if they are struggling with a part of a lesson, they trust that I will pick up on that by interpreting the body language of the quiet students and by listening to the concerns of the vocal ones. Flexibility shows them that I am paying attention and that I care.

I went back and analyzed the possible reasons that one group of students responded so well and the other didn't. For one thing, the second period students had a natural camaraderie that allowed people to respond honestly in class. In contrast, there was a little friction among the third period students. They did not feel all that comfortable around one another, and these insecurities kept them from being themselves. Another important factor was that second period also had four older students who were repeating 9th grade English. These four were the first ones to laugh at the satire. I think their maturity level, combined with the camaraderie of the class, helped everyone enjoy the satire instead of being afraid of laughing at something that other people might see as dumb.

Going back and analyzing this experience enabled me to choose future assignments that I could tailor to suit the personalities of both classes. This analysis would have been impossible if I had responded emotionally to the situation in third period. It would have been extremely easy to get angry with third period for not responding as second period did, and even easier to get frustrated with myself for being a "bad" teacher, unable to reach her students. I chose a calmer, more rational path. This enabled me to focus on my ultimate objective (exposing students to different types of writing styles). Calm thinking helped me offer choices to both classes, engage the students in their learning, and maintain a positive learning environment—and at the same time, meet my own needs.

Questions for Reflection

1. How do you make teaching your art?
2. What steps do you take to rekindle your students' love of learning?
3. Give an example of a time you showed empathy to a student, and explain how the student responded.
4. How do you assess what your students already know about a topic so that you can begin a lesson at the appropriate level?
5. How do you maintain your love for your chosen subject matter?
6. Describe a lesson that you designed to connect to your students' immediate lives.
7. What do you do when the students just aren't "getting it"?

Epilogue

To be what we are, and to become what we are capable of becoming, is the only end of life.

—Robert Louis Stevenson

I always feel as though I'm flying through the air when I am able to give of myself and my gifts are received gratefully. Like most people, I am much more willing to give when I believe that my offerings will not be rebuffed. So I create a classroom atmosphere where giving and receiving are the norm. My students are accustomed to seeing me consistently give them my time, energy, and care. This makes them willing to respond to me in kind.

I also work to help my students see my class as a place where they will be accepted in every way. Their ideas, their behavior, and their appearance will not be belittled in my class. This encourages them to behave in an accepting way toward their classmates and predisposes them to be open to new ideas introduced in the curriculum or in discussion. I value English as a worthwhile subject for my students and me to pursue. If I can create an environment where the students feel an element of this same valuation, then I have done my job.

Teaching has to start with the desire to have a smoothly functioning class. As a professional, you know that kids need to understand and feel safe in their environment in order to function. The reason I have been able to consistently maintain a comfortable educational atmosphere where my students learn the material and know they are able to learn more is because I care about my students and make that care explicit to them. The design of my four guidelines and my reactions to discipline problems is rooted in this care and organized by logic. Students flourish when they see the logic of a teacher's reactions to them and feel that their teacher is reacting to them because he or she is trying to help them develop into better human beings.

Go ahead and give students your time, energy, and care. Recognize the unique qualities and experience you bring to the classroom. See that person you are in your mind's eye, and let that person teach the class. Embrace the truly significant, truly rewarding, truly transformative power of your chosen profession.

Index

Figures are indicated with an italicized *f* following the page number.

About the Author

Katy Ridnouer has taught students ranging from age 5 to 55 in ethnically and economically diverse classrooms. She has taught English in a public high school and a public middle school and is a member of the faculty at Central Piedmont Community College, where she has taught in a high school diploma program, in a developmental English program, and in a teacher training program. She has been a reading specialist, English teacher, and journalism teacher at a private school for students with learning disabilities, and has taught in a high school equivalency program on the Cheyenne River Reservation. She has also worked with students one-on-one in a tutoring center and in private practice.

Katy earned a Bachelor of Arts degree in English and a Master of Education degree at George Mason University in Fairfax, Virginia. She lives in Matthews, North Carolina, with her husband and three sons. You may contact her at katyr@carolina.rr.com.

Related ASCD Products

For the most up-to-date information about ASCD resources,
go to www.ascd.org. ASCD stock numbers are noted in parentheses.

Audio

Making Good Choices: Developing Responsibility, Respect, and Self Discipline
by Richard Curwin and Allen Mendler (audiotape: #204217; CD: #504351)
Secrets of the Teenage Brain: Reaching and Teaching Today's Teenagers by
Sheryl Feinstein (CD: #505281)
*Winning Over Challenging Students: Five Sessions from the ASCD 2006 Annual
Conference* (CD: #506148)

Mixed Media

Classroom Management Professional Inquiry Kit by Robert Hanson (8 activity
folders and a videotape) (#998059)

Online Professional Development

Go to ASCD's Home Page (http://www.ascd.org) and click on Professional
Development to find ASCD's online courses *Classroom Management: Building
Relationships for Better Learning, Managing Challenging Behavior,* and *The
Reflective Educator.*

Print Products

Beyond Discipline: From Compliance to Community, 10th Anniversary Edition
by Alfie Kohn (#106033)
Classroom Management That Works: Research-Based Strategies for Every Teacher
by Robert J. Marzano, Jana S. Marzano, and Debra J. Pickering (#103027)
Educational Leadership, April 2005: The Adolescent Learner (#105034)
Educational Leadership, March 2003: Creating Caring Schools (#103032)
A Handbook for Classroom Management That Works by Robert J. Marzano,
Barbara B. Gaddy, Maria C. Foseid, Mark P. Foseid, and Jana S. Marzano
(#105012)
*The Soul of Education: Helping Students Find Connection, Compassion, and
Character at School* by Rachael Kessler (#100045)

Video

Classroom Management That Works (3-part series with facilitator's guide)
(DVD: #604038; videotape: #404038)
High Schools at Work: Creating Student-Centered Learning (3-part series with
facilitator's guide) (DVD: #606117; videotape: # 406117)

For more information, visit us on the World Wide Web (http://www.ascd.org),
send an e-mail message to member@ascd.org, call the ASCD Service Center
(1-800-933-ASCD or 703-578-9600, then press 2), send a fax to 703-575-5400, or
write to Information Services, ASCD, 1703 N. Beauregard St., Alexandria, VA
22311-1714 USA.